THE CREATIVE SYSTEMS
PERSONALITY TYPOLOGY

Also by Charles Johnston:

The Creative Imperative: Human Growth and Planetary Evolution

Necessary Wisdom: Meeting the Challenge of a New Cultural Maturity Pattern and Reality: A Brief Introduction to Creative Systems Theory

The Power of Diversity: An Introduction to the Creative Systems Personality Typology

An Evolutionary History of Music: Introducing Creative Systems Theory Through the Language of Sound (DVD)

Quick and Dirty Answers to the Biggest of Questions: Creative Systems Theory Explains What It Is All About (Really)

Cultural Maturity: A Guidebook for the Future

Hope and the Future: Confronting Today's Crisis of Purpose

On the Evolution of Intimacy: A Brief Exploration into the Past, Present, and Future of Gender and Love

Rethinking How We Think: Integrative Meta-Perspective and the Cognitive "Growing Up" on Which Our Future Depends

Creative Systems Theory: A Comprehensive Theory of Purpose, Change, and Interrelationship in Human Systems (with Particular Pertinence to Un-Understanding the Times We Live in and the Tasks Ahead for the Species)

Perspective and Guidance for a Time of Deep Discord: Why We See Such Extreme Social and Political Polarization – and What We Can Do About It

Insight: Creative Systems Theory's Radical New Picture of Human Possibility

Intelligence's Creative Multiplicity: And Its Critical Role in the Future of Understanding

Online:

Author/professional page: www.CharlesJohnstonMD.com
The Institute for Creative Development: www.CreativeSystems.org
The Creative Systems Personality Typology: www.CSPTHome.org
An Evolutionary History of Music: www.Evolmusic.org
Cultural Maturity: A Blog for the Future: www.CulturalMaturityBlog.net
Ask the Cultural Psychiatrist YouTube channel: youtube.com/@cjohnston

THE CREATIVE SYSTEMS PERSONALITY TYPOLOGY

Engaging the Generative Roots
of Diversity

CHARLES M. JOHNSTON, MD

The Institute for Creative Development (ICD)

Press Seattle, Washington

Publisher's Cataloging-in-Publication
(Provided by Cassidy Cataloguing Services, Inc.).

Names: Johnston, Charles M., author.

Title: The Creative Systems personality typology : engaging the generative roots of diversity / Charles M. Johnston, MD.

Description: Seattle, Washington : The Institute for Creative Development (ICD) Press, [2023] | Includes bibliographical references and index.

Identifiers: ISBN: 978-1-7342431-4-7 (paperback) | 979-8-9867952-0-1 (ebook) | LCCN: 2022924006

Subjects: LCSH: Typology (Psychology) | Temperament. | Personality. | Self-consciousness (Awareness) | Cultural pluralism--Psychological aspects | Social Evolution

Classification: LCC: BF698.3 .J64 2023 | DDC: 155.264--dc23

The Institute for Creative Development (ICD) Press, Seattle Washington
Copyright @ 2023 by Charles Johnston, MD. All rights reserved. No part of this book may be reproduced, except for review and brief excerpts with attribution, without the written permission of the publisher. Manufactured in the United States of America. For information address The Institute for Creative Development (ICD) Press, 4324 Meridan Ave. M., Seattle , WA 98013, or CJ@creativesystems.org.

Cover design by Safeer Ahmed and Lyn Dillman
Author photo by Brad Kelvin
Library of Congress Control Number: 2022924006
ISBN: 978-1-7342431-4-7
First Printing 2023

THE CREATIVE SYSTEMS PERSONALITY TYPOLOGY

Introduction: Why It Matters	vii
Chapter One: Setting the Conceptual Stage	1
Chapter Two: Early-Axis Temperaments	19
Chapter Three: Middle-Axis Temperaments	34
Chapter Four: Late-Axis Temperaments	50
Chapter Five: Overarching Observations	64
Chapter Six: Illustrative Vignettes	88
Chapter Seven: Experiential Approaches and Comparisons	106
Chapter Eight: Applications with Children	122
Chapter Nine: Advanced Reflections	143
Afterword: A Most Timely Significance	158
Appendix: Creative Systems Theory and the Concept of Cultural Maturity	160
Index	190

INTRODUCTION

Why It Matters

It is startling how different from one another people can be as a function of personality style. Just as startling is how oblivious we can be to such fundamental differences. Living in our different worlds, we pass, barely seeing one another. Or we may recognize that someone is "different" but misinterpret what we see. Personality style bigotry is one of the few kinds of discrimination that people today continue to find acceptable.

Blindness to personality style differences extends beyond everyday interactions. Within academia, attempts to delineate and articulate such differences are not widely acknowledged and are often simply dismissed. And even within spheres such as education and psychology, where we would expect the importance of temperament[1] diversity to be obvious, rarely does it get more than superficial attention.

This book examines what is arguably the most nuanced and sophisticated framework for understanding personality/temperament diversity available. It is a product of Creative Systems Theory (CST),[2] a comprehensive framework for understanding purpose, change, and interrelationship in human systems. Creative Systems Theory was developed over the last fifty years by myself and

---

1   I will use the terms "personality style" and "temperament" interchangeably.

2   See Charles M. Johnston, MD, Creative Systems Theory: A Comprehensive Theory of Purpose, Change, and Interrelationship in Human Systems (with Particular Pertinence to Understanding the Times We Live In and the Tasks Ahead for the Species), 2021, ICD Press.

others at the Institute for Creative Development, a Seattle-based think tank and center for advanced leadership training. The theory offers a way to put understanding of all sorts into systemic context. It brings detail and dynamism to the way we think about developmental processes, from individual growth to the evolution of culture. It also addresses more here-and-now systemic relationships—differences and interconnections that we find between human systems at any one point in time. The Creative Systems Theory Personality Typology is the most elaborated and refined tool in the theory for understanding such here-and-now significance and difference.

The concept of Cultural Maturity, a pivotal notion within Creative Systems Theory, helps us appreciate why a better understanding of personality style/temperament diversity is so important—and of particular importance now and for times ahead. The concept describes how our times demand—and make newly possible—a critical next chapter in how we understand, an essential kind of "growing up" as a species. Cultural Maturity involves changes not only in what we think, but in *how* we think. Such changes make it possible to more consciously and deeply engage the whole of our cognitive complexity, all of the multiple aspects of who we are. An ability to more deeply appreciate personality style/temperament differences follows from these important steps forward.

The importance of better understanding personality diversity has multiple, related layers. As a start, today's loss of past cultural guideposts means that we face a whole new kind of challenge when it comes to questions of identity. We no longer have the same God-given rules to rely on—absolute moral dictates, clear instructions for what it means to be a man or a woman, or unquestioned assumptions about the nature of success. If we are not to be left wandering aimlessly, we need ways to better understand what makes us who we are and how meaning manifests differently in people's lives. A full realization of identity requires that we more effectively grasp both how each of us is unique and how our particular contributions fit into humanity's larger fabric.

Such perspective also helps us understand others more clearly. I've noted that personality style discrimination is one of the few kinds of bias that people continue to find acceptable. As with bigotry of other sorts, people who are different from us easily become psychological "others"—known less for who they are than as reflections of what we find strange and "other" in ourselves. A better knowledge of personality style differences helps us get beyond such common blindnesses.

Appreciating personality style diversity also has critical implications for particular realms of understanding. If we take the time to grasp temperament differences deeply, it can seem hard to imagine, for example, that teachers could teach effectively without such perspective or that psychologists could in any way be of help. Education has made a start toward acknowledging individual differences with attempts to delineate learning styles. But learning style notions rarely capture more than the most surface layers of our diversity. And while psychology has gone a bit further in teasing apart deeper differences, frameworks tend to be limited and not commonly taught. Psychologists today rarely go beyond separating human experience into normality on one hand and various categories of pathology on the other. In missing how richly varied normality can be, they fail to effectively affirm human differences and often end up applying labels that do more harm than good.

Of particular significance in our time, better understanding personality differences also helps us deal more effectively with conflict. More and more often today, social and political discord sets neighbor against neighbor and undermines effective decision-making.[3] Polarized views commonly reflect not only differences of belief, but also differences with regard to which personality style's "reality" is going to prevail. I often draw on the metaphor of a box of

---

3   See Charles M. Johnston, MD, Perspective and Guidance for a Time of Deep Discord—Why We See Such Extreme Social and Political Polarization and What We Can Do About It, 2021, ICD Press.

crayons to communicate how Cultural Maturity's cognitive reordering expands experience. We can think of personality styles as the different hues of crayons in the box. Understanding just how such multi-hued diversity works helps us better address conflicting views.

Expanding on this observation brings us to what ultimately may be the most significant reason for understanding temperament diversity. I've written extensively about how the critical challenges of our time are almost all systemic in nature. Addressing them effectively will require the collaborative input of all the various perspectives that make up the whole of human experience—those of scientists and artists, liberals and conservatives, thinkers and feelers … and on. Successfully engaging the essential tasks before us as a species will require a major leap in our understanding of—and sensitivity to—the very different ways we organize experience.

Reflections from my years leading yearlong trainings at the Institute provide concrete illustration of this most big-picture sort of contribution. I would select participants for programs according to a couple of criteria. People would need to be "up to the task" in the sense of being able to tolerate the complexities we would be addressing. But just as important in the end was personality style. I chose participants so that temperament diversity as the typology describes it was fully represented. One of the things that would most strike people on the first day of trainings was how different many of the individuals in the room were from the people they were most used to spending time with. Because these were universally impressive individuals,

Most immediately, having that particular kind of diversity in the room was powerful at a personal level. A person may never be a jazz musician, a professional football player, or an advertising executive; but if one can begin to understand what might make such people who they are—and better, even slightly embody their felt realities—their presence can help one more deeply engage experience's full systemic complexity. Just having this degree of diversity in the room in itself provided important learnings. To help make these learnings more conscious, partway through the year I would engage the group in a hands-on exploration of the Creative Systems Personality Typology.

Having that kind of diversity in the room also became essential for our shared work together. The mosaic of realities that personality style differences represent supported the collaborative efforts needed to address the deeply systemic questions these emerging culturally mature leaders were there to engage. Near the end of the training, I would have participants divide themselves into small think tank teams to work on the future of spécifie demains—government, business, education, science, religion, and so on. By that time they had come to recognize that choosing like-minded team members was not the right approach if they wanted culturally mature results. If participants' teams were going to be most powerfully creative, they would need the contributions of each basic temperament group.

The Creative Systems Personality Typology provides a way to understand not just the specific strengths and weaknesses of personality styles, but also how different styles can best work together. It also offers an encompassing framework for understanding how personality diversity interplays with other kinds of human difference—such as age, gender, and ethnic/racial diversity. It has particular significance for its power as a tool for supporting the kind of creative collaboration on which a healthy future will more and more depend.

A few brief words of introduction help give a feel for the typology's general approach. The typology has its basis in an observation central to Creative Systems Theory, one that makes sense given the audacity of our species' toolmaking, meaning-making prowess. Creative Systems Theory describes how human cognition is ordered "creatively." It is structured to support and drive innovation. (In Chapter One, we will look at how the theory uses the word "creative" in an unusually encompassing way.) The typology goes on to delineate how we can understand personality differences in terms of the aspects of cognition's creative/generative complexity a person most draws upon. Putting the box-of-crayons metaphor in motion, each hue reflects native affinity with ways of thinking, feeling, and perceiving that come with particular periods in formative process—spanning from generativity's germinal beginnings, to the bringing of new possibility into manifest form, to a time of finishing and completion.

We can recognize this relationship between formative sensibilities and temperament in the goings on of daily life. Within a business, for example, the most germinal ways of knowing stand out with the wild innovators and nerdy "eggheads" over in research and development. We encounter more manifest cognitive patterns with the engineers, managers, and hands-on workers who make sure new discoveries are practical and then turn them into tangible products. And we find more finishing and polishing capacities with the financial, design, and marketing types who take care of money matters and make changes that will support products being attractive to buyers and widely available. Different temperaments have strongest relationship to particular parts of formative process. And different parts of formative process draw on particular aspects of who we are that cause us to see the world in predictably different, creatively related ways.

Chapter One in the book more deeply examines the conceptual underpinnings of the typology. It expands on how our toolmaking, meaning-making, *creative* natures means that such diversity might be predicted. It also highlights recognitions that are key to using the typology effectively.

Chapters Two through Four address the three main temperament constellations in the theory ("axes," to use the theory's language) and examine their multiple manifestations. Chapter Two looks at the various "Early-Axis" personality styles, those that draw preferentially on the beginning aspects of human generativity. Chapter Three addresses "Middle-Axis" personality styles, those that derive meaning and effectiveness by engaging more middle-stage sensibilities. And Chapter Four turns to "Late-Axis" temperaments, those that most reflect the stages of formative process that bring generativity to completion.

The book's remaining chapters turn to more overarching observations. Chapter Five provides additional conceptual detail important to effectively applying the typology. Chapter Six presents a series of vignettes that highlight the challenges and particular richnesses of the various major personality style patterns. Chapter Seven showcases experiential approaches that can be used to introduce the typology and offers comparisons that can help deepen understanding. Chapter Eight examines how the typology can be applied to work with children. And Chapter Nine offers some concluding observations that will be of particular interest to those who wish to apply the typology in professional settings.

The Appendix provides a more extended introduction to Creative Systems Theory and the concept of Cultural Maturity for those who are conceptually inclined.

My hope is that by the book's conclusion you will have gained a solid sense of the typology and the means to put it into practice. If the book has been successful, the perspective it provides will seem striking and radical. And at the same time, its contribution should feel like common sense.

CHAPTER ONE

Setting the Conceptual Stage

Lucretius famously observed that "What is food for one man is to the other poison." While we might think this a problem, in fact it is a good thing. Personality style differences have helped support the diversity of skills and ways of thinking that societies require to function effectively. Wouldn't it be a mess if everyone wanted the same job or if everyone thought like an engineer, like an artist, like a religious leader, or like a politician?

The Creative Systems Personality Typology takes this kind of observation significantly further. It describes how the capacities that characterize particular personality styles reflect different aspects of human cognition's rich and generative mechanisms.

To understand how this is so we could just dive in and turn to the next few chapters' descriptions of personality styles and their characteristics (and you can do this). But engaging these ideas at all deeply will require having a solid foundation for the book's reflections. Further conceptual background is needed if we are to fully understand the differences we see. And certainly a more complete introduction is necessary if we are to appreciate the significance of those differences. Some patience in getting started will be well rewarded.

Creative Systems Theory

We should first step back and look more closely at Creative Systems Theory's general approach. The theory takes as its conceptual starting point the question of just what most defines us as humans. Some people have described this as our ability for language, others our capacity for conceptual abstraction or for complex social relationships. Creative Systems Theory argues that our great capacity to create underlies each of these more concrete attributes. We are toolmakers, and makers not just of things but also of ideas and social structures, and, of particular pertinence to our tasks here, makers of meaning.

The word "creative" as applied in Creative Systems Theory stretches well beyond our usual use of the term. It concerns art no more than science, nor the language of imagination any more than hard logic. But once its meaning is expanded sufficiently, the term captures quite well the heart of needed changes in how we understand. It also serves powerfully as an organizing concept for more detailed conception. CST delineates how creative organization provides a pattern language for making sense of how and why we see our personal and collective worlds in the ways that we do, how those ways evolve over time, and why in our time they may be evolving in the ways that they seem to be.

Creative Systems Theory concepts address how human systems grow and interrelate—human systems of all sorts: individuals, families, communities, institutions, and cultures. In the process, they provide big-picture perspective for understanding why we humans can perceive in strikingly different and often contradictory ways. This includes why we think in different ways at particular points developmentally (whether in our personal lives, in relationships, or at different stages in culture's evolution)—what the theory calls creative Patterning in Time. It also includes why we see our worlds in the different ways that we do at specific points in time—what it calls creative Patterning in Space. With this later kind of concept the theory gives greatest attention to personality style differences—the focus of the Creative Systems Personality Typology.

Personality Style and a Creative Frame

Making sense of how the theory approaches temperament begins with a couple of observations that I pointed toward in the Introduction. First is how human formative processes of all sorts progress through a related sequence of stages. We could call them creation's incubation, inspiration, perspiration, and finishing and polishing stages—or to use formal CST language, Pre-Axis, Early-Axis, Middle-Axis, and Late-Axis.

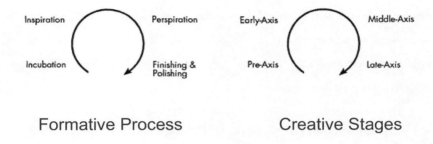

Fig. 1-1. Formative Process and Creative Stages

Second is the striking recognition that we see a related kind of creative patterning with here-and-now systemic differences. The various personality styles, from Early-Axis to Late-Axis, are most gifted in relationship to different stages in formative process and the sensibilities needed to support that stage's creative tasks.[1]

Early-Axis individuals have greatest natural affinity with more "inspiration stage" sensibilities. The various Early-Axis temperament types include people most drawn to experience that involves new possibility. Earlies often contribute as artists, as innovators in the sciences, in work with young children, or as leaders in the information revolution. Think Albert Einstein, Georgia O'Keeffe, or Steve Jobs.

Middle-Axis individuals have greatest association with more "perspiration stage" sensibilities. The various Middle-Axis temperaments are most in their element with activities that involve commitment and heart. Middles often contribute as teachers, as managers in business, as ministers, in the military, in

---

[1] I will address how Pre-Axial personality dynamics represent a special case in modern times in Chapter Nine.

athletics, or in government. Think George Washington, Mother Teresa, or Muhammad Ali.

With Late-Axis individuals "finishing and polishing" sensibilities come to the fore. Values such as worldliness, intellect, style, and material success commonly stand out. Lates often contribute as entrepreneurs and business executives, in academia, as political leaders, as artists of more classical sensibility, and in entertainment and the media. Think John Kennedy, Leonard Bernstein, or Julia Roberts.

A Play of Polarities and Intelligence's Creative Multiplicity

Key to understanding personality styles as described by the typology is the recognition that we are talking not just about differences in beliefs or behavior, but different ways of organizing experience. A couple of approaches that the theory uses to describe the workings of formative process inform the typology's understanding of temperament.

The first approach turns to the role of polarity. Creative Systems Theory describes how we see a predictable sequence of polar juxtapositions over the course of any human formative process.

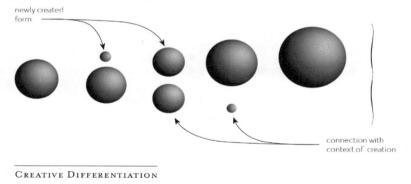

CREATIVE DIFFERENTIATION

Fig. 1-2. Polarity and Creative Differentiation

Creative differentiation manifests as an evolving interplay of polar relationships. Figure 1-2 depicts this progression. Before creative differentiation begins, we find an unbroken wholeness. Early-Axis brings the budding-off of first possibility. With Middle-Axis and the struggle into manifest form, poles exist in near equal balance. Finally, with the finishing-and-polishing tasks of Late-Axis, the more form-defined pole becomes preeminent. We will see how personality qualities reflect the polar juxtapositions that underlie the realties of particular temperaments.

To fully grasp the implications of this first approach, we need to add a recognition about the inherent nature of polar relationships. Drawing on language from psychology, any polarity juxtaposes qualities that are more archetypally feminine (softer, more germinal) with qualities of a more archetypally masculine (harder, more manifest) sort. People can find the use of gender-linked language problematical as today we better appreciate the role each kind of quality plays in each of us. I will often speak instead of polar juxtapositions having more "left-hand" and more "right-hand" aspects. But the more psychological terminology highlights something essential that follows from a creative frame—the ultimately "procreative" workings of the relationships that order human experience. It also helps bring essential nuance to our understanding of personality style differences.

The second approach will similarly prove pivotal in pages ahead. It shifts our attention to intelligence's multiple aspects and how together they make us who we are. Creative Systems Theory observes that our multiple ways of knowing function not merely as options on a menu; they work together to support and drive formative process. The theory describes how each stage in any creative/formative process has strongest association with a particular aspect of intelligence's creative power and its particular way of ordering reality. Put most simply, with Pre-Axis, body intelligence predominates; with Early-Axis the intelligence of the imagination steps forefront (with body intelligence still making a major contribution); with Middle-Axis, emotional intelligence plays the larger role; and with Late-Axis, intelligence's rational dimension becomes most defining. Figure 1-3 introduces CST's more formal intelligence language.

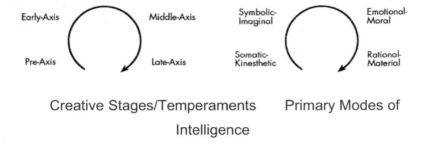

Creative Stages/Temperaments   Primary Modes of Intelligence

Fig.1-3. Axial Realities and Modes of Intelligence[2]

With personality styles, what we find is again analogous. The Creative Systems Personality Typology describes how we can think of personality style differences in terms of the specific intelligences (really specific combinations of intelligences) that people of different temperaments preferentially draw on. The more explicitly creative Early-Axis types draw most directly on symbolic/imaginal intelligence (with some also drawing in major ways on body intelligence). Middle-Axis types, with their more concrete and applied sensibilities draw most deeply on emotional/moral intelligence. And Late-Axis types with their greater capacity for detail and refinement draw most on rational/material intelligence.

These two ways of understanding creative organization—the workings of polarity in formative process and the role of intelligence's creative

---

[2] In fact the result is more interesting than just one intelligence for each stage. In Chapter Nine we will look at how each kind of intelligence manifests in particular, more limited ways at each stage. But with each stage, one kind of intelligence plays the dominant role. For a detailed look at intelligence and formative process see Charles M. Johnston, MD, Intelligence's Creative Multiplicity: And Its Critical Role in the Future of Understanding, 2023, ICD Press.

multiplicity—will each be central to observations in chapters ahead. They will help bring needed detail to understanding not only how people are different, but also why—to just what makes each of us "tick" in the particular ways that we do.

Cultural Maturity and Temperament

Besides a basic understanding of creative organization, deeply engaging the Creative Systems Personality Typology also requires at least a solid beginning sense of the concept of Cultural Maturity. The typology is not inordinately complex, and its structure has a pleasing elegance that follows directly from the theory's more general approach to understanding. But it does demand that we think in new ways.

We need to have at least begun to engage Cultural Maturity's changes if we are to effectively grasp temperament's rich diversity. This recognition helps clarify why historically we have done so poorly when it comes to appreciating personality style differences. Without Cultural Maturity's cognitive reordering we at best recognize only superficial differences. And we are likely to attribute that which we observe to other people's ignorance or inadequacy. The experience of difference easily translates into polarized projection—most often of a denigrating, although also sometimes of an idealizing sort.[3] Cultural Maturity's cognitive changes make it newly possible to consciously hold the complexity of our human differences—to not be overwhelmed by them, and to most powerfully and effectively draw on those differences.

To better understand how this is so, developmental perspective again provides a way in. Any human developmental process in fact has two halves. The first half—what I've highlighted with this chapter's brief look at polarity—

---

3   I've described the demonizing sort of projection that can result in bigotry. But polarized projections can also produce envy and result in giving other temperaments undo power.

is defined primarily by differentiation. We recognize creative differentiation with individual psychological development in how the first half of life is most concerned with the establishment of identity—of ourselves as distinct beings. The second half of any creative/formative process involves further differentiation; but even more, it is defined by integrative dynamics. We see this kind of more integrative mechanism in how our later years can bring with them the ability to get our minds around juxtapositions that we have experienced previously as mutually exclusive either/ors—such as good versus evil, certainty versus uncertainty, or masculine versus feminine. Such "bridging" of polarities is key to how our later years bring the potential for greater wisdom.[4] The concept of Cultural Maturity proposes that we are now seeing the beginnings of something parallel in the developmental dynamics of culture.

We can also think of Cultural Maturity's integrative changes in terms of the cognitive reordering that produces them. Creative Systems Theory describes how the mature stages in any formative process are marked by the ability to stand back more fully from, and at once to engage more deeply, the whole of our cognitive complexity. The new, more complete and systemic kind of vantage that results—what the theory calls Integrative Meta-perspective[5]— offers that we might more effectively grasp systemic relationships of all sorts. The term is a bit of a mouthful, but it addresses what is involved with Cultural Maturity's cognitive reordering quite precisely. The notion also sheds important light on temperament differences. I've noted the theory's claim that people of different temperaments are different because they preferentially inhabit—and derive their gifts from—different parts of cognition's complexity. (Remember

---

4   "Bridging" in this sense is not about averaging or joining as we might conventionally assume, but rather about thinking more systemically—why I put the term in quotes.

5   See Rethinking How We Think: Integrative Meta-Perspective and the Cognitive "Growing Up" on Which Our Future Depends, 2020, ICD Press.

that box of crayons.) If accurate, Integrative Meta-perspective should make this fact newly visible.

Further Delineations

Distinguishing between Early-Axis, Middle-Axis, and Late-Axis personality constellations is just a start with regards to the kinds of discernments needed to effectively tease apart temperament differences. Four further kinds of distinction have particular importance with the typology.

First, we also need to distinguish more vertical—Upper Pole and Lower Pole—differences. Within any major personality style group we find people who are more Upper in their sensibilities, more "lofty" (whether spiritually or intellectually), and others who are more Lower, more "down to earth." For example, the personality structures of a business executive would tend to be more Upper Pole and that of a blue-collar worker more Lower Pole.

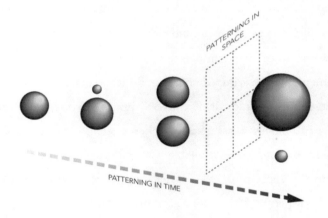

Fig. 1-4. Vertical and Horizontal Distinctions

With the second kind of distinction we delineate more horizontal—Inner Aspect and Outer Aspect—dynamics. In a similar way we find some people who are more Inner, more internally focused or reflective, and others who are more Outer, more expressive or outgoing. The personality structure of a priest is likely to draw more heavily on Inner Aspect qualities, while that of a news commentator would likely draw more on Outer Aspects. Figure 1-4 depicts vertical and horizontal dynamics as they exist within particular temperament axes.

The three variables of Axis, Pole, and Aspect describe the twelve basic temperament constellations in the theory. We could speak of one person as an Early/Upper/Outer, another as a Middle/Lower/Inner, and another as a Late/Lower/Outer.

A further kind of distinction is more quantitative. It draws on the Creative Systems Theory concept of Capacitance. Capacitance describes how much of the stuff of life a system can take in before becoming overwhelmed—think of a balloon that will pop if stretched too far. The same personality style constellation will manifest in very different ways depending on a person's Capacitance. Each of the twelve basic temperament groups include individuals who have high Capacitance and individuals with low Capacitance.[6]

A last kind of distinction is less central to how the typology defines temperament, but it has important behavioral and conceptual implications. The theory delineates what it calls Creative Symptoms. Symptoms in this sense are protective mechanisms that manifest when systems are challenged in ways that push them beyond their available Capacitance. The concept of Creative Symptoms is important because it helps us appreciate potential ways that the viewpoints of people with particular temperaments can become distorted. It is also significant conceptually for how it helps us get beyond the limitations of frameworks that see differences and limitations only in terms of pathology.

---

[6] Capacitance is an example of what the theory calls a Whole-System Patterning Concept. In contrast to observations that reflect creative differentiation such as Patterning in Time and Patterning in Space notions, they measure characteristics of systems as living wholes.

Creative Symptoms may function internally by blocking avenues of effect (depression and rigidity being examples), or interpersonally by diminishing the potency of the challenge (for example being combative or undermining). They may protect us by moving us above the challenge (e.g., intellectualization), dropping us below it (e.g., taking a victim posture), moving us inside it (e.g., becoming aloof), or taking us beyond it (e.g., busying oneself)—or by doing more than one of these simultaneously. Creative Symptoms can be part of an ongoing way of relating to the bigness of the world or responses to specific kinds and intensities of challenge.

Creative Systems Theory combines these multiple kinds of distinction—Axis, Pole, Aspect, Capacitance, and Symptom—with developmental (Patterning in Time) notions to produce a detailed picture of how different people at different times and places organize experience and make sense of their worlds. With future chapters, I will further fill out each of these notions. In the three chapters immediately ahead, I will take time with the particulars of how these variables manifest with each temperament Axis. In Chapter Five, I will go into greater depth with regard to how these distinctions interplay to make the experience of any time and place particular. And in Chapter Nine, I will address in more detail how the picture that results helps fill out common ideas about psychopathology.

More on Polarity's Procreative Symmetry

A closer look at the generative symmetry I touched on earlier helps bring needed subtlety to observations. I've described how polarities in human systems juxtapose qualities that are more archetypally feminine (softer, more germinal) with qualities that are more archetypally masculine (harder, more manifest). This "procreative" relationship orders concepts at every level in the theory. For example, we see it over the course of creative/formative processes. The first half of any such process begins in a more archetypally feminine, left-hand reality of germinal mystery and progresses toward a more archetypally masculine, right-hand manifest reality of finished form (with the second half providing maturity's more integrative picture).

With regard to temperament, we see a related progression as we move from Early-Axis to Middle-Axis to Late-Axis personality styles. Of the various temperament constellations, Earlies tend most to embody the archetypally feminine, while Lates tend more to embody the archetypally masculine. With Middles, left-hand and right-hand sensibilities exist in near equal, isometric balance. And vertical and horizontal dynamics similarly reflect this kind of generative symmetry. Lower Pole and Inner Aspect sensibilities draw more on the archetypal feminine; Upper Pole and Outer Aspect sensibilities draw more on the archetypal masculine. We can thus think of Early/Lower/Inner as the most archetypal feminine of personality styles and Later/Upper/Outer as the most archetypally masculine.[7] In Chapter Nine, I will describe how we experience these evolving relationships in the body. They are not just abstract concepts.

A related kind of observation proves powerful when it comes to tying temperament to the tasks of Cultural Maturity. Creative Systems Theory identifies three kinds of polar fallacies, basic ways that our thinking can stop short of culturally mature understanding. It calls them Unity Fallacies, Separation Fallacies, and Compromise Fallacies. Unity Fallacies fall off the left-hand, more archetypally feminine side of the road. (We often find them with more spiritual, romantic, humanistic, and liberal/progressive beliefs.) Separation Fallacies fall off the right-hand, more archetypally masculine side of

---

[7] This generative symmetry as it manifests in the horizontal helps clarify an important distinction. A person might confuse Inner and Outer with the more familiar juxtaposing of introverts and extroverts. While the notions are related, Inner and Outer reflect a more differentiated kind of observation. Each axis has a similar number of Inners and Outers. But because of this generative symmetry, roughly two-thirds of Earlies would be described as introverts (though some of the most outrageously extroverted people are also Earlies). And roughly two-thirds of Lates would be described as extroverts (though, similarly, some of the most sensitive of introverts are Lates).

the road. (We commonly see them with more materialist, rationalist, libertarian, and conservative worldviews.) And Compromise Fallacies straddle the white line in the middle.

In Chapter Five, I will expand on the basic notion and tie it specifically to temperament. As we might predict, Earlies tend to be particularly vulnerable to Unity Fallacies, while Lates more commonly fall for Separation Fallacies. And Uppers and Lowers, Inner and Outers are predictably vulnerable to different kinds of fallacies consistent with their right-hand or left-hand leanings.

Dilemmas, Complexities, and Common Confusions

Some practical observations provide essential guidance in getting started. Right off, we need to acknowledge a necessary dilemma. It follows from the way each of us, by virtue of being human, most embodies one of the personality constellations that I will be describing. Avoiding bias therefore can be a challenge. We need to have made solid progress in learning to step back from and more deeply engage our internal complexities if we are to effectively make sense of this more in-the-world kind of complexity.

We also need to appreciate how temperaments exist along continua. While for the sake of simplicity we can talk in terms of categories—Early, Middle, and Late personality "types"—they are more akin to the colors on a spectrum. When we say a color is "green," for example, at the same time we know that there are lots of different greens, indeed that there is no absolute line that makes one color blue-green and another greenish blue. It is the same with vertical and horizontal dynamics. There is no such thing as a purely Upper or purely Inner personality. We are always dealing with interplays between Upper and Lower Poles, Inner and Outer Aspects. To honor the subtleties of our differences, we need to think in terms of dynamic balances.

The most common mistake for people new to Creative Systems personality concepts is to view "later" personality style as somehow more evolved than "earlier" ones. It is important to remember that while the theory uses similar language to describe creative stages and personality styles, they are separate concepts. Each of us goes through the same sequence of creative realities over the course of our development (and within any endeavor we undertake). And at the same time, different people at the same developmental stage and with the same Capacitance have special affinities for the qualities with which a particular stage imbues reality. This distinction becomes particularly important when it comes to the relationship of Cultural Maturity and temperament. Given necessary Capacitance, each personality style/temperament constellation is equally capable of culturally mature perspective. No personality style has a leg up when it comes to Cultural Maturity. In chapters ahead, we will examine the particular contributions that people with specific temperaments can bring to culturally mature understanding and leadership.

Finally, we need to always keep in mind that we are dealing not simply with behaviors, but with organizing dynamics. There can be great overlap between axes with regard to any particular behavioral characteristic. For example, we find strong intellects in any axis and very creative or deeply feeling people in each as well. While I will often talk in terms of common professions or characteristic beliefs, these can only be pointers. Major exceptions exist to every such behavioral generality. Indeed, the exceptions are often where the most interesting learnings lie. I am introduced to a business executive and expect to meet a Late, and instead encounter an Early. I meet a sculptor and expect to find an Early and instead the person is a Middle. We can also learn from situations where professions and beliefs juxtapose in ways that might seem contradictory. People who become police officers and people who become criminals, for example, often have related personality styles. Personality style constellations are best thought of as "realities" or territories of experience.

How the Typology is Unique

In Chapter Nine I will address how the typology's contribution compares and contrasts with other approaches to thinking about human differences. There are ways in which the Creative Systems Personality Typology is unusual and also ways in which it is specifically unique. For now, I'll simply make the claim that, whichever is the case, Creative Systems Theory's approach takes us important steps beyond more familiar frameworks.

The typology is at least unusual in the way it draws on the whole of intelligence. Arguably any framework that begins to effectively address personality differences will do so to some extent. But the typology engages intelligence's creative multiplicity consciously and with particular depth. I've described how we can think of the CSPT equally well as a framework for understanding differences in how people think, feel, imagine, and live in their bodies.

Taking a moment to reflect on the role of body intelligence in the typology's discernments highlights the major significance of this accomplishment. With each axis description, I will make reference to differences of a bodily sort. It is a fact that could make the framework immediately suspect in certain people's eyes. But it turns out that body cues provide one of the best ways to tease apart tricky personality distinctions. Personality style is only one contributor to bodily life, but its influence is sufficiently strong that I can pretty accurately determine temperament from bodily cues alone. I can sit in a café, watch people come in the door, and guess correctly the larger portion of the time.

Importantly, the cues I would draw on involve more than just bodily structure. Ultimately they concern how a person lives in their body. That includes how a person moves. It also includes where in one's tissues a person carries the greatest bodily charge. For example Earlies tend to carry their charge closer to the bodily core, Lates closer to the surface, while Middles concentrate their charge in the "heart and guts" realms between.[8] It is another topic that I will address in more detail in Chapter Nine.

Ways in which the typology is more specifically unique start with its application of a creative frame in describing pattern. The typology is also unique in being part of a larger, more overarching conceptual framework. I've described how Creative Systems Theory's comprehensive picture of purpose, change, and interrelationship in human systems includes concepts that address both developmental context—what we observe with Patterning in Time distinctions—and the more here-and-now kind of context we find with the typology. This additional kind of uniqueness becomes particularly provocative with the parallels I've described in how these two kinds of discernments are understood and how it is possible to apply the same kind of creative concepts and language with each.[9]

A unique attribute of Creative Systems Theory more generally ultimately underlies the typology's conceptual power. I will describe it in detail in the Appendix. Our times are challenging us to move beyond machine models when addressing living systems. We are needing to find ways to think in more "living" terms—and more specifically, in ways that better address the particular kind of life we are by virtue of being human. The theory's application of a creative frame with its dynamically evolving, relational picture provides the needed conceptual leap. The Creative Systems Personality Typology applies the way a creative frame helps us address living interrelationship in living terms to the dynamics of human difference. This doesn't mean that the typology's concepts cannot be used in unhelpful ways. But when applied well, they will most often

---

8   It is difficult to find language to speak about the body in other than physical terms given the limited degree most people are in touch with their bodies in modern times. In using the word "charge" in this way, I'm referring to where different people most feel life and excitation in their bodies.

9   In Chapter Five I will reflect briefly on how these parallels were first observed and the key role their recognition played in the typology's origins.

crease our appreciation for the unique life of systems we wish to understand.[10]

One consequence of this last difference has particular significance when it comes to personality style differences. The theory effectively addresses a common initial objection, one we confront with any temperament framework. People can assume that CSPT ideas are "just another set of boxes to put people in." Creative Systems Theory reminds us that there are two equally dangerous ways to fall off the road when encountering human differences. We can put people in categories that diminish our appreciation for their complexity (at the extreme, we can be bigots). But just as dangerously we can ignore differences, in the process dismissing what makes a person unique and limiting our capacity for effective communication. A creative frame's more fully systemic kind of perspective helps us understand difference in ways that specifically support the fact that we are alive, and human.

The CSPT and Culturally Mature Leadership

A sophisticated understanding of personality style differences—both the gifts and limitations that come with particular ways of being in the world—is today becoming increasingly essential. This is so with challenges of every sort, from finding identity in the absence of familiar cultural handholds, to seeking what is needed for healthy and fulfilling love, to addressing the newly systemic demands of the contemporary workplace, to the broader tasks of collective decision-making. In each case, while understanding temperament characteristics necessarily stretches us, it also makes new options possible.

---

10   I've noted that the way I use the word "creative" in Creative Systems Theory requires that we go beyond how we might usually apply the term. It is the same with the word "systems." More conventionally, systems language is used in one of two ways. Systems engineers and systems scientists use it to refer to complex interactions in mechanical systems. Those of more spiritual or wholistic bent may use the term to emphasize interconnectedness, at the extreme to argue for ultimate oneness. The word "systems" as used in Creative Systems Theory has a fundamentally different meaning. It refers to living wholes and the differences and interrelationships that make them alive. And more specifically it refers to these differences and interrelations as they order our lives as human beings. (Applying the language of polar fallacies, the two more familiar ways we might think of systems lead, respectively, to Separation Fallacies and Unity Fallacies.)

We can frame the result in terms of leadership. Cultural Maturity is ultimately about leadership—in ourselves and in the world. The growing need for culturally mature leadership highlights the power and importance of understanding temperament differences. Using the box-of-crayons metaphor, effective, culturally mature leadership requires an appreciation for one's own specific "crayon," both one's particular temperament's significance in diversity as a whole and the blindnesses it can produce. And especially when collaboration is required, sensitivity to other people's specific gifts and vulnerabilities becomes similarly essential. We need a solid sense of how "crayons" relate and also how we can best draw on such diversity and complexity when confronting critical creative challenges.

You can think of your engagement with the observations in chapters ahead in terms of leadership. If you find these notions useful, at the least you will have at your disposal an important and practical set of leadership tools. And there are more conceptual leadership implications, ones pertinent to understanding the times we live in and realizing the kinds of thinking needed if we are to advance effectively as a species. Finding these notions of value supports the Creative Systems Theory observation that human intelligence organizes creatively and provides evidence for Cultural Maturity's idea of a needed new chapter in culture's developmental story.[11]

---

[11] See Charles M. Johnston, MD. Insight: Creative Systems Theory's Radical New Picture of Human Possibility, 2022, ICD Press.

CHAPTER TWO

Early-Axis Temperament Patterns

Clockwise from upper left: Anais Nin:P.B. Rage, Wikimedia; Steve Jobs: Matthew Yohe, Wikimedia; Janis Joplin: Wikimedia Commmpons; Kurt Cobain: P.B. Rage, Wikimedia.

Early-Axis temperaments reflect a special affinity with the inspiration stage in formative process—that period when the buds of new creation first find their way into the world of the manifest. Earlies tend to draw most deeply on the intelligences of the imagination and of the body, ways of knowing most tied to beginnings and possibilities. Of all temperaments, the archetypal feminine makes the strongest contribution in the personalities of Earlies. With Earlies, it is often their uniqueness that most stands out, how comfortable they are marching to the beat of their own drum.

Quotes, Occupations, and People

Following are a few quotes that capture Early-Axis sensibilities and values:

I'll play it first and tell you what it is later.
—Miles Davis

The most regretful people… are those… who felt their creative power restive and uprising, and gave it neither power nor time.
—Mary Oliver

I am interested in God's thoughts; the rest are details.
—Albert Einstein

It is life near the bone where it is sweetest.
—Henry David Thoreau

I've always wanted to be someone, but now I see I should have been more specific.
—Lily Tomlin

I don't say we all ought to misbehave, but we ought to look as if we could.
—Orson Welles

Physicists are the Peter Pans of the human race.
—physicist I.I. Rabi

Not all who wander are lost.
—JRR Tolkien

In the haunted house of life, art is the only stair that doesn't creak.
—Tom Robbins

When one tugs at a single thing in nature, he finds it attached to the rest of the world.
—John Muir

The road of excess leads to the palace of wisdom.
—William Blake

THE CREATIVE SYSTEMS PERSONALITY TYPOLOGY

Everything is miraculous. It is miraculous that one does not melt in one's bath.
—Pablo Picasso

Where do we find Earlies? Often they work with young children (a grade school teacher, a day-care worker). Frequently they make contributions in the arts—as visual artists (particularly painters of more abstract inclination and sculptors), dancers (especially those whose aesthetic tends toward the improvisational), musicians (most jazz musicians, many rock and roll musicians, and some classical musicians), writers (often poets and most writers of science fiction), or film directors. Earlies also make important contributions in mathematics and the sciences. Although the larger number of scientists are Lates, many of science's major innovators have been Earlies—particularly in physics, mathematics, and the neurosciences. Biologists are also often Earlies, as are many anthropologists, geologists, and archeologists. Recently, Earlies have starred in the high-tech revolution. (Steve Jobs, Bill Gates, and Elon Musk are all Earlies.) Humorists are often Earlies (think Groucho Marx or Robin Williams). So are many of the best chefs. Most people who teach reflective techniques such as meditation and yoga are also Earlies. (It is Earlies who are most attracted to things spiritual, particularly practices with roots in Early-Axis cultures.)

A few other particularly notable Earlies: Leonardo da Vinci, Georgia O'Keeffe, Rainer Maria Rilke, Mary Cassatt, Stephen Hawking, Carl Jung, Isadora Duncan, Jonathan Winters, Ingmar Bergman, Antoine de Saint-Exupéry, May Sarton, Gregory Bateson, Pablo Neruda, Anaïs Nin, Howard Hughes, David Attenborough, Alan Watts, John Coltrane, Wes Anderson, Jackson Pollack, Margaret Atwood, Alexander Calder, Boris Karloff, Vincent van Gogh, Emmett Kelly (the American clown), John Lithgow, Jack Kerouac, Jules Verne, Daniel Day Lewis, Bob Dylan, Annie Lennox, Oliver Sacks, August Rodin, Alfred Hitchcock, Taylor Swift, cartoonist Gary Larson, Robert Oppenheimer, Frank Zappa, Nikola Tesla, J. R.R. Tolkien, Marlon Brando,

Johnny Depp, Janis Joplin, Jack Nicholson, Joni Mitchell, William Blake, John Lennon, Edgar Allen Poe, Mick Jagger, Lisa Kudrow, Cass Elliot (of the Mamas and the Papas), George R.R. Martin (of Game of Thrones fame), Shaun White (the snowboarder), Billie Eilish, and Mrs. Saunders (my kindergarten teacher). More notorious Earlies include Charles Manson, David Kaczynski (the Unabomber), and Rasputin.

This listing skews toward the more manifest Early-Axis types. This is in no way to imply that they have greatest importance. As is the case with every axis, Uppers and Outers are most in the world and thus tend to be most visible. It is only with the more universally manifest world of Late-Axis personality structures that we see Lower/Inner personalities acknowledged historically, and even then they are underrepresented. Mrs. Saunders is the only pronounced Early/Lower/Inner in this list.[1]

Defining Intelligences and Characteristic Qualities

While some Earlies have exceptional rational capacities, the more germinal aspects of intelligence's creative multiplicity will most often play the major role. Earlies, more than any other temperament, draw on the imaginal—the language of symbol, myth, and metaphor (for the modern Early, as experienced within the rational/material context of today's Late-Axis culture). The magical and imaginative dimensions of this intelligence most predominate with Early/Uppers and Early/Outers. The mythical and mystery-centered dimensions tend to hold sway in the psyches of Early/Lowers and

---

[1] A related reason helps explain why we see more men than women with this listing and with previous quotes. In part it is because of the simple fact that historically men have had more visible roles. But differences are particularly pronounced with Earlies because of the strong influence of archetypal feminine sensibilities. In a world where Middle/Uppers and Lates have greatest influence, it tends to be only the Earlies who have the most archetypallly masculine in their makeup who are widely recognized. (See Chapter Five for reflections on the relationship between temperament and gender.)

Early/Inners. Edgar Allan Poe captured the inner world of the Early when he wrote: "All that we see or seem is a dream within a dream."

Body intelligence can also have a particularly strong role with Early-Axis temperaments. Early/Lowers in particular tend to be more comfortable in their bodies than other temperaments and derive particular fulfillment through bodily experience. Indeed, for many Earlies, body and spirit can be hard to distinguish. I think of Walt Whitman's familiar words, "I sing the body electric."

Earlies tend to find special fascination with questions of meaning. And often the contributions of Earlies are quite visionary. Arthur C. Clark observed that, "The purpose of the universe is the perpetual astonishment of mankind." The greatest contributions of Earlies often derive from their ability to discern underlying principles and patterns.

On meeting an Early, one is often first stuck by a childlike quality. In keeping with their relationship to creative development's earliest stages, Early-Axis people tend to have a special appreciation for childhood sensibilities, both in themselves and in the world around them. A certain non-conformism is a common Early Axis trait, but its origin is less rebellion than a mistrust of—and even ignorance of—established convention.

Of all axes, Earlies tend to be most comfortable with situations where the unknown yet outweighs the known. Ursula K. Le Guin once observed that, "The only thing that makes life possible is permanent intolerable uncertainty: not knowing what comes next." Stephen Hawking proposed that, "Intelligence is the ability to adapt to change."

Earlies can take great joy in the nonsensical and contradictory. Lewis Carroll famous words from Through the Looking Glass come to mind: "'Contrariwise,' continued Tweedledee, 'if it was so, it might be; and if it were so, it would be: but as it isn't, it ain't. That's logic.'" They can also be drawn to the ineffable and even mysterious. Paul Klee once reflected, "I am not at all comprehensible in the world. I dwell with the dead as well as with the unborn, and somewhat closer to the heart of creation than is usual. And not nearly close enough."

In spite of their particular connection in the more imaginative aspects of intelligence, what is often most striking about the Early-Axis person is humility and patience. Richard Feynman counseled that, "The first principle is that you must not fool yourself, and you are the easiest person to fool." Words from poet Rainer Maria Rilke help make the connection: "Make your ego porous. Will is of little importance, complaining is nothing, fame is nothing."

Earlies also often feel a more immediate connection with nature than other temperaments, and greater comfort with solitude (whether alone in nature or just with themselves). I am reminded of these familiar words from Yeats' poem "The Lake Isle of Innisfree:"

> *I will arise and go now, and go to Innisfree,*
> *And a small cabin build there, of clay and wattles made;*
> *Nine bean-rows will I have there, a hive for the honeybee,*
> *And live alone in the bee-loud glade.*

An important consequence of the strong contribution from the archetypally feminine is that Earlies, of all temperaments, tend to have the most permeable boundary structures. While this boundary permeability can be the Early's undoing, it is also the source of many of the Early's great gifts and strengths—such as intuitiveness and attentiveness to interconnections. Abstract painter Wassily Kandinsky once observed that, "Men of sensitivity are like much-played violins which vibrate at each touch of the bow." With Earlies, we often find greater fluidity than with other temperaments when it comes to gender identity and sexuality. People who describe themselves as "non-binary" are often Earlies.

Poles and Aspects

These attributes take expression in characteristic ways with various Early-Axis patterns. With Early/Uppers, qualities such as imagination, charisma, spiritual and artistic sensitivity, and inventiveness predominate. Early/Uppers make manifest the sensibilities of the "magical child."

Where Inner aspects predominate, the Early/Upper's artistry is most internal. We find Early/Upper/Inner sensibilities with many visual artists (Georgia O'Keefe), certain poets (Anaïs Nin), and some musicians (Joni Mitchell). I think of the words of Pablo Neruda—"My obligation is this: to be transparent." We recognize them too with people who are drawn to the more ascendant and ascetic of spiritual practices.

Where Early/Upper/Outer aspects are strongest, the Early/Upper's imaginativeness may manifest through more dramatic forms of artistic expression (think John Lennon) or through scientific or technical invention (as with Einstein, Nikola Tesla, or Steve Jobs). Often the intellect makes a major contribution. It is here that we find the notorious "mad professor."

With Early/Lowers, attributes like connection to nature and mystery, a deep capacity to nurture, and spontaneity are most prominent. We see embodied simultaneously the playful aspects of the child (as opposed to the numinous and magical) and the child's connection with the primordial. (Think Jonathan Winters or Emmet Kelly). Often Early/Lowers find a comfort with darkness not seen with other temperaments. I think of Antoine de Saint-Exupéry's description of night as "when words fade and things come alive." Biologists, anthropologists, and archeologists often have Early/Lower elements in their personalities, as do many pathologists and undertakers. Goth aesthetics have their roots in Early/Lower sensibilities.

With Early/Lower/Outers we are often most struck by their capacity for abandon. Spontaneity and the ability to improvise come easily. Early/Lower/Outers often manifest the artistic in particularly dramatic ways.

Here, mythically, we find the wild man and wild woman. This is the most common temperament pattern for the more outrageous of rock and roll musicians (Janis Joplin or Mick Jagger). It is also where we find actors such as Jack Nicholson, Willem Dafoe and Johnny Depp. Salvador Dali once exclaimed, "I do not take drugs—I am drugs."

Early/Lower/Outer is also a temperament we see with athletes, particularly those notable for having a wild or original style. Athletes of the extreme sport sort, such as snowboarder Shaun White often have significant amounts of Early/Lower/Outer in their makeup. Early/Lower/Outer qualities are also common with athletes in sports where size and abandon together can provide an advantage. Football running back Marshawn Lynch—know affectionately as "beast mode" in my home town—makes a good example.[2]

With Early/Lower/Inners, qualities like the ability to nurture and a delight in the mysterious predominate. Early/Lower/Inners also often manifest through artistic expression, but most frequently of a more personal sort. Certain more reflective musicians are also Early/Lower/Inners. I think of Kurt Cobain. Blues artists (Howlin' Wolf or B. B. King) tend to combine Early/Lower/Inner and Early/Lower/Outer qualities. Many Early/Lower/Inners contribute through work with children—attracted either to selflessly serving the children's "magic" or to the possibility of living immersed in the unformed. Here we also find some of the best chefs. We also find many people who work directly with the body, such as massage therapists. Many Early/Lower/Inners also find fulfillment in work with animals. Early/Lower/Inners in particular would appreciate these words of poet Izumi Shikibu: "As I dig for wild orchids in the autumn fields, it is the deeply bedded root that I desire, not the flower."

---

[2] We also often see at least a touch of Early/Lower/Outer in Middle-Axis athletes who are particularly known for the improvisation and artistry that they bring to their sport (such as Michael Jordan or Lionel Messi).

Figure 2-1 uses some common qualities to map the four Early-Axis quadrants:

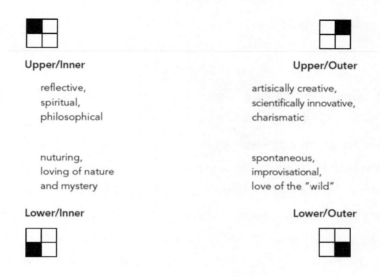

Fig. 2-1. Early-Axis Poles and Aspects

Limitations and Symptoms

Common limitations of Earlies parallel their strengths. Earlies often have a difficult time finding satisfaction in the traditional work world. They tend to like more freedom than most jobs provide and can be a bit too eccentric or original in their thinking to fit in well. They can also lack the facility with detail and comfort with repetitive tasks that the workplace can demand.

Weaknesses of Earlies frequently follow from that permeability of boundary structure. The Early-Axis person can seem fragile or frail and often does poorly in contexts that involve significant conflict or competition. Earlies can lack the thick skin needed for the often hardball realities of modern life.

Earlies are much more likely than Middles or Lates to feel awkward in social situations. Even the more expressive of Earlies can seem introverted and a bit "nerdy." Earlies also frequently find societally expected forms of commitment either challenging or not of real interest. Relationship can be very important to the Early, but it must somehow support and complement the Early's creative sensibilities to be long lasting.

Earlies can also have problems distinguishing between dreams and dreams made manifest. Or they recognize the difference, but are simply not good at carrying tasks to completion. A recent newspaper column jokingly referred to an obviously Early-Axis person as "planning impaired."

When Symptoms manifest in an ongoing way with Early/Upper dynamics (when the Early/Upper's available Capacitance is chronically insufficient for the challenges of daily life), the Early/Upper's charisma can transform into something closer to grandiosity. There can also be a touch of paranoia. If this charisma attracts followers (people to connect with within a reality the Early defines), the Early person can be quite magical and charming. But where follows are lacking—and often as an adult they will be—the Early can feel frightened and alone. Where the dynamic is more inward, the grandiosity tends to be spiritual rather than personality focused.

Where Symptoms manifest in an ongoing way with Early/Lower dynamics, we often find a marked tendency toward depression. I think of the ongoing struggles of musical genius Brian Wilson (of Beach Boys fame). The spark of inspiration can be swallowed up before it has a chance to appear. Particularly with more Early/Lower/Inner patterns, dependency is also common. Where with Early/Upper we can see the grandiosely self-centered child, here we see the needy child. A magical causality again operates, but now it is centered on an external agent such as a charismatic individual or a group (like a religious cult). The Early/Lower's rudimentary boundary capacity can also take expression in avoidance of social contact or antisocial behavior that keeps others at bay. It can also manifest in behavior that undermines others and through acting in suffocating ways in relationships with one's children.

Earlies and the Body

Earlies often look young for their age. The bodies of Early/Uppers tend to be thin and unusually flexible. Appearance can range from the waif-like look of Joni Mitchell to the gangly, awkward child visage of Lyle Lovett. The major parts of a person's charge are carried in the inner, "magical" layers of the upper chest, face. The eyes of Early/Uppers can seem particularly animated or intense.

Early/Upper people tend to be taller than the norm. This is likely a function of the fact that Earlies most often have a later-than-usual onset of puberty and, with this, a delay in closing of the skeletal growth plates. Earlies often continue growing well into their late teens and early twenties. Note this description of Nobel physicist and colleague Theodore B. Taylor: "She found him attractive—tall, gangling with a broad forehead, a somewhat parted chin, and great thoughtful brown eyes, which often seemed to be focusing on something no one else could see."[3] With extreme Early/Upper dynamics, tissues and movements can take on a brittle quality. As a person moves beyond an age where childlike narcissism is appropriate, this brittleness can become the dominant body characteristic..

With Early/Lower temperaments, we see several different body patterns, each characterized by a tendency toward unboundedness and the carrying of charge primarily in the belly and pelvis. With Early/Lower/Inner dynamics, we see two patterns. In the first, the person tends toward being thin and gaunt, a "hungry child." In the other, there is more pudginess, like a child yet to lose its baby fat. (Think Jonathan Winters.) Here there can be significant obesity, the bulk often serving as a covert boundary. With more Early/Lower/Outer dynamics, there can again be considerable body mass, but it tends to be more

---

[3] From John McPhee, The Curve of Binding Energy: A Journey into the Awesome and Alarming World of Theodore B. Taylor, 1994, Farrar, Straus, and Giroux. Dr. Taylor was a participant in a think tank on nuclear wast disposal that I led many years back.

animated. (Think Orson Wells or Alfred Hitchcock.) And with Early/Lower/Outer athletes, mass can be not only animated, but also packaged in a way that is solidly structured and fit.

Phrases and Associations

When I do personality style workshops, I often ask people to write down phrases and associations that capture the experience of their particular temperament. Here are some statements from the mouths of Earlies:

It can help if I have others around who can take my wild brainstormings and put them into reality.

I've often named the cars I've owned. The ones I remember most fondly are not the ones that ran best, but those with special or quirky personalities.

I am most happy when things have a sense of almost sacred balance.

I can feel least alone when I am by myself.

My hair has a mind of its own.

People sometimes think I am sad or depressed when actually I am just deep inside myself, and in fact most happy.

In having children, I particularly love the almost vegetative state of pregnancy and very early mothering.

I love things primordial: the roar of the ocean, the musky smell that lingers after sex.

Earlies and the Future

I've mentioned that no temperament has a leg up when it comes to culturally mature understanding. Each is equally capable of high Capacitance, and thus capable also of bringing Integrative Meta-perspective to how they think and act. But Earlies often feel a particularly strong connection to future-related concerns. Most people we consider visionaries are Earlies, as are many people who think of themselves as futurists. I have a favorite future-related quote from Early poet Theodore Roethke on my writing room wall: "What we need is more people who specialize in the impossible."

At the same time, characteristic blindnesses of Earlies can get in the way of the Early's ability to address the future in useful ways. Earlies can be particularly vulnerable to utopian thinking, of either the more techno-utopian or spiritually utopian sort. Of all temperaments, they are the most apt to fall for cynical or outright dystopian thinking. Their native comfort with uncertainty can predispose them to postmodern traps in which they confuse anything-goes assumptions with the future's needed more complete kind of understanding. And because Earlies often identify with the Early-Axis developmental times in culture, they can be prone to confusing the thinking of times past with culturally mature understanding.[4] Of all temperaments, Earlies are the most likely to fall for Unity Fallacies.

An Early Vignette

With each Axis-specific chapter, I will end with a vignette that expands on the importance of that chapter's particular insights. Just for fun, each draws from experiences from my own life. (Chapter Six includes an array of further vignettes.)

---

[4] As with the equating of spiritual perspectives such as those of classical Buddhism with the kind of thinking needed going forward.

The first comes from my relationship with the colleague who for many years worked most closely with me on the development of the CSPT. It concerns how she first came to appreciate the typology's particular contribution. She had previously taught university courses on conflict resolution and communication. These courses included some basic ideas about personality differences. She was now taking part in one of my extended trainings.

My colleague had two daughters. One daughter had a Late-Axis personality style not too different from her own (my colleague's temperament spanned Middle/Upper/Inner and Late/Upper/Inner). The second daughter was decidedly Early and also quite Inner. She frequently left my colleague baffled, and often they bumped heads.

After one particularly unsettling interaction with her Early daughter, my colleague asked if she could explore her confusion in the training. She and the Early-Axis daughter had argued, and my colleague had tried to apply the tools that she so often taught others for dealing with such circumstances. She made direct eye contact with her daughter, asked her to describe her feelings, and then fed back what she heard. The daughter responded by breaking into tears, running upstairs to her bedroom, and slamming the door. My colleague started to go upstairs and try again, but then somehow sensed that this would be a mistake.

When she shared this story in the training, I proposed that while her approach would likely have worked well with a Late and adequately with a Middle, it wasn't likely to work with an Early/Inner. Asking her daughter to describe her feelings and then repeating back her words would imply that words could capture what she felt (which for an Early will rarely be the case). And direct eye contact could easily feel like intimidation. Predictably, instead of feeling seen and heard with my colleague's well-intentioned strategy, the daughter had felt the opposite.

I suggested to my colleague that she try a very different approach if her daughter again retreated upstairs in response to conflict. First she should let some time go by. Then she should walk quietly up the stairs and knock gently on the daughter's door. After a pause she should then walk quietly into the room, and without making eye contact, sit on the floor with her back to the bed. She should sit there for a couple minutes without saying anything. Then she should simply whisper "I love you" and return downstairs.

My colleague promised to try this approach and report back. The result: The daughter came back downstairs after about a half hour and said nothing. Indeed, the topic of concern never came up again. Somehow it had been resolved. This experience convinced my colleague that she needed ways of thinking that could address personality differences at a deeper level than those she had learned and had been teaching.

CHAPTER THREE

Middle-Axis Temperament Patterns

Clockwise from upper left: Martin Luther King, Jr.; Margaret Thatcher: Marion S. Trikosko, Wikimedia; Babe Ruth; Mother Teresa: Manfredo Ferrari, Wikimedia.

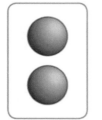

Middle-Axis temperaments most strongly embody "perspiration" stage sensibilities—those we find with the period when new creation struggles into crude, but now solid, manifestation. While all intelligences play roles with Middle sensibility, Middles draw with particular strength on emotional intelligence. Polarity plays a particularly explicit role in the personalities of Middles, with the cognitive structures of Middles characterized by a near balance of at once opposing and colluding polar qualities. We've seen how Earlies identify most with the first improvisational sparks of creation. Middles find greatest meaning turning sparks into usable fire. The Middle-Axis fire both does essential work and warms the hearth of community.

Quotes, Occupations, and People

Here are a few words of familiar Middles:
Here are a few words of familiar Middles:

A man can only do what he can do. But if he does that each day, he can sleep at night and do it again the next day.
—Albert Schweitzer

One of the oldest human needs is having someone wonder where you are when you don't come home at night.
—Margaret Mead

In war there is no substitute for victory.
—Douglas MacArthur

You've got to make it happen; its not just going to happen.
—Dolly Parton

The better part of a man's life consists of his friendships.
—Abraham Lincoln,

I only regret that I have but one life to give for my country.
—Nathan Hale

Great works are performed not by great strength, but by perseverance.
—Samuel Johnson

The only thing that seems eternal and natural in motherhood is ambivalence.
—Jane Lazarre (American writer)

Opportunity is missed by most people because it is dressed in overalls and looks like hard work.
—Thomas Edison

It is the function of vice to keep virtue within reasonable bounds.
—Samual Butler

When I am good I am very, very good, but when I am bad I am better.
—Mae West

Everybody loves an outlaw. At least they never forget 'em.
Jesse James

Where are we likely to find people with Middle-Axis temperaments? Middles often become teachers, engineers, small-business owners, government workers, librarians, writers, managers, bankers, military officers and soldiers, athletes and coaches, union bosses, ministers or priests, physicians (about an equal balance of Middle/Upper and Late/Upper), or politicians (a similar balance). Much of the "real work" in society is done by Middles. Police officers and firefighters, nurses and social workers, truck drivers, machinists and auto mechanics, carpenters and electricians, forest rangers and fishers, food service workers, security guards and sales people are commonly Middles.

Musicians are also often Middles (particularly country, rock, gospel, punk, and rap musicians, and some classical musicians). In addition, Middles make up the greater portion of stay-at-home parents. It is with Middle-Axis that we find the strongest identification with home, family, and community. Women who think of themselves first as wives and mothers are commonly Middles, as are the most devoted husbands and fathers. Middle-Axis individuals of both sexes frequently play strong roles in their neighborhoods, churches, and local social service organizations.

Observing some of the activities Middles often take part in helps bring attention to Middles who may be less visible. The most committed spectators of sports such as football, baseball, basketball, or soccer tend to be Middles as are the larger number of participants in such sports. Middles also often take part in outdoor activities such as fishing, hunting, boating, horseback riding, skiing, golf, bowling, swimming, or tennis. Middles are the most likely to be found playing music together with friends, taking part in community theater, or singing in the church choir. More solitary Middle activities include gardening, cooking, knitting and sewing.

Some additional better known Middles include Eleanor Roosevelt, Abraham Lincoln, Mother Teresa, Martin Luther King, Bruce Springsteen, Margaret Thatcher, Will Rogers, Joe Louis, Billy Graham, Babe Ruth, Serena Williams, Andrew Carnegie, Frederick Douglas, Florence Nightingale, Ernest Shackleton, Arnold Palmer, LeBron James, Colin Powell, Roy Rogers, Dale Evans, Aretha Franklin, Clint Eastwood, Bella Abzug, Julia Child, Dale Earnhardt, Queen Victoria, Johnny Cash, Jimmy Carter, Chris Evert, J. Edgar Hoover, Richard Prior, Thurgood Marshall, Ice Cube (the rapper), Amy Schumer, Archie Bunker (as played by Carroll O'Connor), Hulk Hogan, Jimmy Kimmel, Johnny Rotten (the punk rocker), Cesar Chavez, Golda Meir, Mary Lou Retton, George Washington, Rush Limbaugh, Queen Elizabeth, Boris Yeltzin, Betty Friedan, Norman Schwarzkopf, Willie Nelson, Jackie Robinson, Marie Dressler (in the movie Tugboat Annie), Jay Leno, Jimmy Hoffa, both George H.W. and Barbara Bush, and TV characters Fred and Ethel Mertz. More notorious Middles include Joseph Stalin, Adolf Hitler, Joseph McCarthy, Ma Barker, and, as above, Jesse James.

Again, Lower Pole figures—particularly Lower/Inners—are not well represented in this list. But Middle/Lower is where we find many of the most important, if unheralded, figures in our lives: the neighborhood bus driver or mail carrier, the friend who is there no matter what, the parent who puts a special note in a child's lunchbox. The larger portion of "essential workers" during the Covid pandemic were Middles.

Defining Intelligences and Characteristic Qualities

Emotional-moral intelligence, the intelligence of heart and guts (as it manifests within Late-Axis culture) orders the Middle's world. The stuff of the heart holds sway in Middle/Inner and Middle/Lower temperaments, where the archetypally feminine is strongest. Harder sensibilities, the stuff of guts and fortitude, dominate with Middle/Upper and Middle/Outer temperaments.

Rational intelligence can play a strong role with Middles, but it tends to be of the more practical, problem-solving sort. The larger portion of engineers are Middles. More imaginal and body sensibilities can also be strongly present, but the imaginal tends to be concerned more with craft than art, and the body mostly with more concrete manifestations such as hands-on work and athletic endeavors. Middles tend to keep the more germinal and erotic aspects of imaginal and body intelligence at arm's length.

Middle-Axis dynamics move us firmly into the human dimension. Early-Axis and Late-Axis realities are each in their own ways abstracted from the personal. Early-Axis deals with the pre-personal reality of creative buddings; Late-Axis deals with the post-personal world of the intellectual, the social, and the material. Middle-Axis puts us right in the middle, engaged directly in the tasks of mortal existence.

Throughout Middle-Axis we see a strong capacity for hard work, deep emotional and moral convictions, and the ability to persevere and to sacrifice when necessary. In the words of Winston Churchill, "This is a lesson: Never give in—never, never, never, never." Middles are attracted to the basic. "Home is where the heart is." Loyalty is an especially valued trait. The phrase "salt of the earth" would rarely be used except to refer to a Middle-Axis person.

Middle-Axis creativity tends to be less that of glaring originality than the application of new possibility to what exists. The most skilled craftspeople whatever the medium tend to be Middles. With some notable exceptions, Middle-Axis people tend to be incrementalists rather than leapers. "A bird in the hand is worth two in the bush" is a Middle-Axis sentiment." So is describing oneself as "a workhorse rather than a show horse." Middle-Axis is where we find the best day-to-day, hands-on problem solvers, whether in the halls of Congress, in the office, in the home, or on the factory floor.

Middles tend to respect strong moral fiber and emphasize the importance of responsibility. They often speak with a bluntness not found with other temperaments. Harry Truman once observed, "I never give them hell. I just tell them the truth and they think it is hell." Middle-Axis personalities tend toward the traditional in their leanings (though this does not necessarily translate to conservative). Humility and unpretentiousness are often strong values (though bravado can prevail with Outer aspects). It is not uncommon for Middle-Axis parents to warn of the dangers of getting "too big for your britches." Teddy Roosevelt said it well for the political sphere: "Speak softly and carry a big stick."

You will note the tendency toward sayings and homilies in these descriptions. Homilies are a peculiarly Middle-Axis art form—"a stitch in time saves nine," "people who live in glass houses shouldn't throw stones," "haste makes waste," etc. Middles tend to love good stories and to be adept at telling them. Some relevant adage often makes the point.

Middle-Axis dynamics juxtapose opposites in near equal balance. Like two ends of a teeter-totter, polar tendencies simultaneously battle and collude. In the Middle-Axis psyche, strength struggles with weakness, thoughts with feelings, good with evil, domination with submission, control with abandon, honor with dishonor. Meaning for a Middle is a reflection of timely balance (though often of a conflicted sort) between such isometrically interplaying forces. The reward for this creative push-pull is the realization of substance and the satisfaction of a job well done.

Middle-Axis wisdom tends to be of the practical, common sense sort. This can be decidedly down to earth. A Czech proverb (here Middle both in Patterning in Time and Patterning in Space) counsels, "Do not pick your wife at a dance, but in the field among the harvesters." It can also be more elevated as in Reinhold Niebuhr's well known prayer, "God, give us grace to accept with serenity the things we cannot change, the courage to change the things that should be changed, and the wisdom to know the difference."

Poles and Aspects

Words we might associate with Middle/Upper personalities include fortitude, authority, dominance, practicality, courage, uprightness, fairness, and moral conviction. Middle/Uppers tend to be good problem solvers. They are also often strong leaders.

With Middle/Upper/Outers this capacity for leadership frequently takes the form of formal organizational leadership—the leadership of politicians, captains of industry (though where the gift of an industry leader is primarily with finance, more Late/Upper/Outer quantities commonly dominate), coaches, or military officers. We hear both the fortitude and the generosity of spirit often found with Middle/Upper/Outer sentiments in these words of George Patton: "Wars may be fought with weapons, but they are won by men. It is the spirit of the men who follow and the man who leads that gives the victory."

Middle/Upper/Inner leadership tends to manifest in ways that are more personal and interactional. Upper/Inner sensibilities are common in teachers, managers, and religious leaders. Middle/Upper/Inner leadership commonly has a strong ethical component. It is compassionate, but also resolute. Benjamin Franklin observed that, "Sin is not hurtful because it is forbidden, but it is forbidden because it is hurtful."

People of Middle/Lower temperament are commonly known for their perseverance and loyalty, and for their capacity to support or nurture. Middle/Lowers tend to place great importance on relationship. For Middle/Lower/Inners, the most defining relationships tend to be with friends, family, and immediate community. Besides being good parents, Middle/Lower/Inners often contribute as teachers (particularly of children and adolescents), as social workers, as behind-the-counter salespeople, in nursing, or in the food industry. They are also the people who bring together neighborhood potlucks and organize the annual kiddie parade.

For Middle/Lower/Outers, the key relationships tend to be with community in a broader sense, with team members, or even more broadly, with one's ethnic group or nation. Middle/Lower/Outers commonly become police officers, soldiers, farmers, carpenters, and professional athletes. Middle/Lower/Outers can be capable of particularly strong bonds of allegiance. They are the buddies on the battlefield who will die for you.

Middle/Lowers do much of the hands-on protecting and heavy lifting of society. Henry Wadsworth Longfellow's familiar poem "The Village Blacksmith" reflects Middle/Lower values:

> *Under the spreading chest-nut tree*
> *The village smithy stands;*
> *The Smith a mighty man is he,*
> *With large and sinewy hands,*
> *And the muscles of his brawny arms*
> *Are strong as iron bands.*
> *His hair is crisp, and black, and long.*

His face is like the tan;
His brow is wet with honest sweat,
He earns whate'er he can,
And looks the whole world in the face,
For he owes not any man.

Middles are often known for having a sometimes odd or irreverent sense of humor. I remember a Middle/Upper engineer client of mine arriving at a session wearing a T-shirt that read, "An optimist thinks a glass is half full. A pessimist thinks a glass is half empty. An engineer knows that the glass is twice as large as it needs to be." Middle/Lower/Outers in particular enjoy humor of the jostling camaraderie or put-down sort. Jack Dempsey once offered the following piece of practical wisdom: "Some night you'll catch a punch and all of a sudden you'll see three guys in the ring around you. Pick out the one in the middle and hit him, because he is the one who hit you."

Some descriptive words and common qualities for the Middle-Axis quadrants are shown in Figure 3-1.

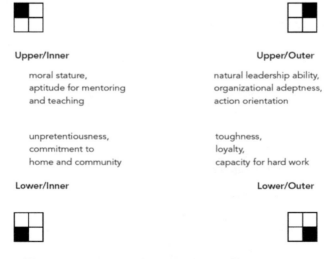

Fig. 3-1. Middle-Axis Poles and Aspects

Limitation and Symptoms

Shortcomings again tend to express the flip side of common strengths. For example, the Middle's great capacity for control can be a major impediment. The Middle/Upper's need to be on top (both of others and his or her own impulses) can make it hard either to surrender authority or to let go of oneself sufficiently to find fulfillment. The Middle/Lower's tendency to feel most safe (and in control) if someone else is in charge can also be limiting. If Middle/Lowers are not careful they can become passive or undermining of authority.

When Capacitance is limited, one kind of shortcoming can prove particularly problematical. The polar tensions inherent to Middle-Axis dynamics may translate into social polarization and even bigotry. What might otherwise be experienced simply as difference is instead felt as a moral threat—in the extreme, of a life or death sort.

Middles can also let themselves be limited by a more everyday sort of threat to self-esteem. Because Middles manifest less of both the intuitive sensitivity common with Early-Axis patterns and the refinement and differentiation found with more Late-Axis sensibilities, their attitudes and beliefs can seem to others (and often to themselves) to be coarse or simplistic. This conclusion can be reinforced by the common Middle-Axis tendency toward concreteness. Middles are notorious for retelling all the details of an event rather than summarizing and abstracting.

Where Symptoms prevail in Middle-Axis, control dynamics become amplified. In Middle/Upper/Inner patterns, this can take expression as ardent moralizing or more personally in harsh self-criticism or compulsiveness. With Middle/Upper/Outer patterns, it can manifest interpersonally in bullying or abuse.

With Middle/Lower/Inner patterns, we can see passivity, undermining behavior, and not infrequently through undermining of oneself, depression. With Middle/Lower/Outer patterns, the struggle from below usually manifests more directly in oppositional tendencies and aggression—or sometimes criminal behavior. The great majority of people in prison are either Middle/Lower/Outers or Early/ Lower/Outers.

The need for occasional release of control can make alcohol and other addictive drugs especially attractive for both Uppers and Lowers, with potential for misuse. And Middle/Lowers in particular can be vulnerable to gambling addiction. Go to either an alcohol or gamblers anonymous meeting, and the larger portion of attendees will be Middles.

Middles and the Body

Middles tend to carry their charge predominantly in the muscles and viscera. This manifests differently for more Upper and Lower, Inner and Outer Patterns. Particularly where more archetypally masculine dynamics play a strong role, the muscle mass in Middle-Axis patterns will often exceed what one would expect just from exercise (the isometric posture keeps the musculature in a state of exertion).

Where Middle/Upper/Outer predominates, mass tends to concentrate in the chest, shoulders and neck. We get a more V-shaped body (particularly in men, but also to a more limited degree with women). With Middle/Upper/Inner dynamics, we tend to see more balance. Commonly we find a more symmetrical, wiry, or blocklike body.

In Middle/Lower personalities, the muscular and visceral layers of the body are again most engaged, but especially with Middle/ Lower/Inner, the focus shifts more to the viscera. Here we may see relative balance, but with charge residing primarily in the stomach, hips, and thighs. We can also again see isometric tension resulting in added mass. Where more Outer aspect dynamics predominate, we can see either a more a more V-shaped often athletic body, or a block-like body, relatively symmetrical but strongly bound.[1]

Words and Associations

Identifying words and phrases given to me by Middles include:

A good education is the key to a productive life. Teachers are our real heroes

Politics has to do with power, who has it and who doesn't.

Never say die.

The caterpillar does all the work and the butterfly gets all the publicity.

Children, family, and God. In these lie life's true riches.

I like people who are plainspoken, people who are unpretentious and forthright.

There are no atheists in foxholes.

Shit or get off the pot.

There is nothing more precious than a good friend

A good leader has to be willing to make tough, often uncomfortable decisions. You will not always be loved, but in the end you will be respected.

I know how to be there for others.

---

1   These descriptions of body dynamics explain why football coaches often pat their players on the butt (something that in other circumstances we would likely find offensive). The gesture engages the Lower Pole of heart-and-guts Middle-Axis sensibility. For business people, who tend more often to be Middle/Uppers or Lates, a handshake provides the needed greater formality and distance.

You play the cards you're dealt.

Few things give me more pleasure than working in my garden.

I can be something of a sentimental packrat—I collect things and then can't throw them out because they remind me of an event or a particular person.

I can be a bit of a bull in a china shop. It is one of my strengths—butting heads a bit can get things to happen—and one of my weaknesses; I can end up locking horns when there might be a better way to handle things.

I'm a strong person emotionally. I can withstand a lot of adversity. And I know how to be there for people.

I have to be careful of what I agree to do, because I'll do it. For good or ill, I'm a person who keeps their commitments.

I'd rather be fishing.

When I buy something, I want it to be well made so it will last a long time.

People can count on me, but I don't like to be taken for granted.

I feel most at home when I am working with my hands—doing carpentry, baking bread, digging in the garden.

It would be very much like me to use my vacation to work on my house.

The old saying, 'the family that prays together, stays together,' makes a lot of sense to me.

I can relate to people with alcohol and drug problems. If I had made some other choices, I could be in their shoes.

If it ain't broke, don't fix it.

I can feel guilty about the stupidest of things. I can even feel guilt about feeling guilty.

A blank sheet of paper scares me.

Talk is cheap.

Middles and the Future

When it comes to the basic tasks of planning, Middles have always had, and will continue to have, a central role. It is here that we find the engineers that design our bridges and power infrastructures. Middles are also our military planners, tasked with being sure we are ready for any future conflict. They also plan their children's lunches.

With regard to culturally mature understanding and leadership, I've emphasized how each axis has equal potential for realizing Integrative Meta-perspective. The Middle's relationship to this task can seem contradictory. In contrast to Earlies who are most likely to think that something new is needed, Middles are more likely to conclude that things are fine as they are. But given a chance to engage culturally mature understanding deeply, Middles can often be the ones who end up with the most solid grasp of its importance and just what it involves.

All this makes sense from how the cognitive processes of Middles work. The failure to recognize that anything new might be needed follows from the conservative nature of Middle-Axis sensibilities. Middles tend not to like circumstances that involve great uncertainty nor conclusions that require thinking in fresh ways. Indeed, where Capacitance is limited, Middles can prefer truths of times well past if they see them as foundational—such as with fundamentalism in the religious sphere, or originalism in the interpreting of laws.

But at the same time there is a characteristic of Middle-Axis sensibility that provides an important advantage when it comes to engaging culturally mature understanding. Middle-Axis cognitive structures share with Integrative Meta-perspective the fact that they include archetypally masculine and archetypally feminine qualities in about equal measure. Because these qualities are set in polar opposition in the Middle's native cognitive makeup, Middles can find culturally mature perspective on first encounter disturbing, often decidedly so. But, with familiarity, the high Capacitance Middle may also particularly appreciate the balance that Integrative Meta-perspective provides. I often describe culturally mature understanding as a needed "new common sense." Many of the people who have come most to recognize Creative Systems Theory's importance and who are today most adept in its application are Middles.

A Middle-Axis Vignette

I'll end these Middle-Axis reflections with another vignette, again from my personal experience. This one comes from quite early in my life.

My temperament is largely Early. In contrast, my father's temperament was pretty much dead-on Middle. In Chapter Six I'll share a vignette that ties this observation together with developmental dynamics. This chapter's example turns to how I came to appreciate our differences and my father's particular contribution as a Middle.

I remember distinctly a conversation I had with my father while sitting together in the car on a fishing trip. I was trying to sort out what was important to me and the directions I might want to take in my life. Like any good Early, I was trying to discern what most inspired me, to discover my "calling." Hoping to get some wise counsel, I asked my father how he had answered that question in his life.

But to my frustration, he kept looking at me like he did not understand what I was asking. I tried presenting the question other ways, but got no further. I knew he was an intelligent person, but his confusion had me wonder if in fact he was not as sharp as I had thought. Finally, he turned to me and said simply, "What I want ultimately is to be 'well used.'" It was clear that "being well used" could mean a lot of different things.

At first I didn't find his answer any more satisfying than a lack of anger. It seemed to miss the point. But over time, I came to realize that he had given a perfect answer for who he was. With the help of the CSPT today I could say he had given a perfect Middle-Axis answer. It is a recognition that has served me well in years since in working with many Middle-Axis clients. I've come to see that my task is to help each person find the kind of life that for them would have them feel most well used. I often share the story about my father. It helps Middles get beyond comparing themselves with others and affirm their sense of where to find meaning in their particular lives.

I've also come to realize how much my father succeeded in his life with "calling" in this particularly Middle-Axis sense. In the later part of his life he worked as a parole and probation officer. As he described it, he got to be father to 150 guys. And he obviously did a very good job. Most every Christmas, four or five ex-cons he had worked with through the years would stop by the house with gifts for my dad. He had very much succeeded in being "well used."

CHAPTER FOUR

Late-Axis Temperament Patterns

Clockwise from upper left: Barbara Walters, Wikimedia; Ted Turner, Wikimedia; Sammy Davis Jr., Wikimedia; Dorothy Hamil, Wikimedia.

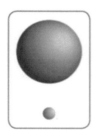

Late-Axis patterns correspond to the finishing and polishing stage in formative process—the developmental period that turns our attention to questions of detail. Rational/material intelligence most orders experience, often bringing particular emphasis to the intellect; but we can also find the emotional and the aesthetic taking strong expression. Because Late-Axis is the most natively Outer of patterns, of all temperaments, Lates tend to function most easily and efficiently in the external world.

Quotes, Occupations, and People

Following are a few words from well-known Lates:

In times of turbulence and change, it is more true than ever that knowledge is power.
—From John F. Kennedy

In a word, I am always busy, which is perhaps the chief reason I am always well.
—Elizabeth Cady Stanton

Science is nothing but trained and organized common sense.
—T.H. Huxley

I rightly conclude that my essence consists of this alone that I am a thinking thing.
—René Descartes

Tis better to have loved and lost, than never to have loved at all.
— Alfred, Lord Tennyson

Look . . . ours is a business of appearances, and it's terribly important to appear to be self-confident . . . the minute you give evidence of doubt, people are going to eat you alive.
—Ted Koppel

I don't do fashion; I am fashion.
—From Coco Chanel

When in doubt, wear red.
—Bill Blass

Reading maketh a full man, conference a ready man, and writing an exact man.
—Francis Bacon

We should all just smell well and enjoy ourselves more.
—Cary Grant

I have seen poor and I have seen rich. Rich is better.
— Sophie Tucker

The true mystery of the world is the visible, not the invisible.
—Oscar Wilde

The universal regard for money is the one hopeful sign in our civilization.
—George Bernard Shaw

To be able to fill leisure intelligently is the last product of civilization.
—Bertrand Russell

Lates often become professors, lawyers, scientists, Wall Street bankers, fiction or non-fiction writers, CEOs, political leaders, architects, economists, interior designers, publishers, hedge fund managers, ballet or modern dancers, editors, theater directors, actors, businesses owners, fashion models, art dealers, classical musicians, orchestra directors, popular singers, advertising executives, television newscasters, playwrights, sales people, marketers, servers at high-end restaurants, financial advisors, or, today, social media influencers. Certain athletes, such as ice skaters and some tennis players can be Lates.

More than with any other axis, various individuals can differ widely in their inclinations. A look to the Creative Function and the defining polarity depicted at this chapter's beginning provides explanation. It is here that we see the greatest natural separation between poles. Within Late-Axis we find the people who are most rational in their perspective, and also those who tend most toward the romantic. We find the people who are most materialistically driven, and at once many of those most committed to artistic and intellectual pursuits where monetary remuneration is often slight. We find the people most aggressively in the world, and also many of those most internal and reflective in their proclivities.

Some other well known Lates include: Carl Sagan, Nancy Pelosi, Frank Sinatra, Nelson Mandela, Barbara Walters, Barack Obama, Julia Roberts, Leonard Bernstein, Woodrow Wilson, Judy Garland, Jerome Powell, Clark Gable, Elizabeth Warren, Audrey Hepburn, Katharine Hepburn, Sammy Davis, Jr., Walter Cronkite, Yo-Yo Ma, Jacques Cousteau, William Shakespeare, Ursula von der Leyen (European Commission President), Hugh Bonneville (of Downton Abbey), Elizabeth Taylor, Jonas Salk, Alistair Cooke, Grace Kelly, Ted Turner, Harry Belafonte, Paul Newman, Gloria Steinem, Harrison Ford, Cornelius Vanderbilt, Will Smith, Johnny Carson, Steve Martin, Chita Rivera, Nicole Kidman, Henry Lewis Gates, Paris Hilton, Peter Lynch, Kenneth Clark, Mikhail Baryshnikov, Peggy Fleming, Shirley MacLaine, Dick Cavett, Bob Hope, William F. Buckley, John Stewart, Donald Trump, Hallie Berry, Sidney Poitier, Jerry Seinfeld, Lena Horn, John D. Rockefeller, Jamie Dimon, Misty Copeland, Kim Kardashian, and Robert Redford. Less savory sorts tend to engage in white collar crime, so are less visible and less often prosecuted than Early and Middle lawbreakers—Michael Milken and Bernie Madoff come to mind, along with those involved in the investment bank excesses of the 2008 financial collapse.

Defining Intelligences and Characteristic Qualities

While rational intelligence takes its clearest expression in the personalities of Lates, emotional intelligence can also present itself in ways that are particularly refined and sometimes dramatic and flamboyant. Imaginal and body intelligence tend to play lesser roles, but their contributions can still be significant, particularly with the more artistic concerns of Lates.

Of all temperaments, Lates tend to manifest most easily and effectively—whether in the sphere of ideas, with professional accomplishment, or with popular notoriety. When we say someone is scholarly or intellectual, most often we are making reference to a Late. And the word "celebrity" more often than not refers to a Late.

More than other temperaments, Lates are also likely to be financially successful. They tend to value external reward. In addition, they are often particularly good with the monetary world's details and complexities. And of all temperaments, Lates are the most natively competitive.

Lates are especially likely to be adept socially. This can take highly formal expression—etiquette and sophistication come naturally to many Lates. Lord Chesterfield observed that, "Politeness and good breeding is absolutely necessary to adorn any, or all, other good qualities or talents." As often, it manifests in a simple ease and comfort in the social arena. Lates commonly have an unusual degree of interpersonal flair. When we say someone has "personality" or "style" we are usually referring to a Late.

Lates can be quite creative, but their creativity tends to be of a different sort than either the whole-cloth originality of Earlies or the more applied creativity of Middles. Late-Axis scientists are likely to be recognized for the precision and detail of their experimental work and for their ability to bring together existing work to reach new conclusions. Late-Axis visual artists, dancers, and musicians most often work from established traditions or written scores and make their primary creative contributions through refinement and subtlety of aesthetic expression.

More than other temperaments, Lates tend to be aware of trends and what is popular. In the academic world, this can manifest in being attuned to the kind of thinking that is most in vogue in a particular discipline. In the wider world, Lates tend to know what is currently fashionable.

Lates tend to be more attentive to physical appearance than other temperaments, We might commonly refer to a Late as looking "smart," "sharp" or "well put together"—our language reflecting the Late's underlying cognitive orientation. It is Late-Axis men who are most likely to be found regularly wearing a suit and tie, and on special occasions a tuxedo. And it is Late-Axis women who are most likely to wear high heels and to feel comfortable attired in a cocktail dress or even a ball gown. Ralph Waldo Emerson reflected on having "heard with admiring submission the experience of the lady who declared that the sense of being perfectly well-dressed gives a feeling of inward tranquility which religion is powerless to bestow." Estée Lauder offered this advice: "Never just 'run out for a few minutes' without looking your best. This is not vanity—it is self-liking."

Poles and Aspects

The qualities that most stand out with Upper Pole, Late-Axis personalities are clarity of thought, verbal facility, and the ability to deal easily and effectively with the material world. (Think Nancy Pelosi or Ted Turner.) Being a Late/Upper gives you the best chance of getting into Harvard or Yale or being hired by a respected law or financial firm.

With Late/Upper/Inners, the more intellectual and literary of these qualities stand out. University professors, scientific researchers, architects, and nonfiction writers commonly have Late/Upper/Inner personalities. Late/Upper/Inner is also where we find the greatest appreciation for sophistication and refinement. In the words of Lady Montague, "Civility costs nothing and buys everything." A diplomat might combine these more intellectual and social Late/Upper/Inner capacities.

With Late/Upper/Outers, more external and material concerns take center stage. It is here that we encounter the people who are most facile with money and the complexities of the business world—executives of larger corporations,

Wall Street professionals, captains of industry of the more finance-oriented sort, and media moguls. We also find "serious" media personalities such as television news commentators. While for Late/Upper/Inners the intellect resides most comfortably in the ivory tower, Late/Upper/Outers apply it to the most worldly of concerns.

With Late/Lower patterns, qualities such as talent, gregariousness, sensuality, and emotional presence often most stand out. (Think Nicole Kidman or Frank Sinatra.) We commonly find Late/Lower sensibilities with people in the performing arts. Late/Lowers often have a rich sense of the dramatic, as well as the smoothness and presence needed to pull it off. Sophia Loren once observed that "sex appeal is fifty percent what you've got, and fifty percent what people think you've got." The major portion of beauty pageant contestants are Late/Lowers. Of all personality groups, Late/Lowers are most likely to enjoy being "on stage."

Where the balance is toward Inner, the dramatic focus highlights emotional and aesthetic nuance. Late/Lower/Inner is the most common personality style of people involved in formal artistic performance—ballet and modern dancers, theater actors. Television and movie personalities are also often Late/Lower/Inners. This is also a common temperament with musicians in the pop music sphere. Novelists along with visual artists of a more realist bent also often find their creative source in Late/Lower/Inner sensibilities, as do interior and fashion designers.[1]

With Late/Lower/Outers we find the people with the greatest capacity to project and be visible. Late/Lower/Outers tend to be successful at marketing and promotion (both of things and themselves). The more glittery and flamboyant of actors and actresses tend to have Late/Lower/Outer

---

[1] Note that even the most Inner of Late-Axis personalities may pursue what might seem Outer pursuits. Because Late dynamics are the most manifest, even sensibilities that are particularly internal may take expression in the world of form. For the same reason, the way even more Lower Pole Lates present themselves can seem quite elevated.

personalities, as do the more packaged and promoted of musicians. In the words of Ethel Merman, "There's no business like show business." More day-to-day, Late/Lower/Outers may work for advertising agencies or sell high-end clothing or real estate.

Some descriptive words and common qualities for the Late-Axis quadrants are shown in Figure 4-1.

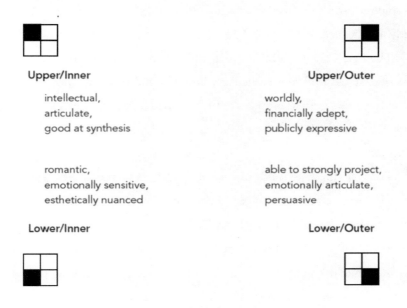

Fig. 4-1. Late-Axis Poles and Aspects

Limitations and Symptoms

Weaknesses again reflect the flip side of common strengths. Lates who are especially intellectual or materialistic can have a difficult time finding real depth of engagement in themselves or emotional closeness with others. It is not so much that they fear these things (as can be the case with Early/Uppers and Middle/Uppers) than that how they live in their bodies may leave them a long way from where needed sensibilities reside.[2]

The competitiveness that often drives achievement for Lates can also be an obstacle. The academic may find it hard to get beyond intellectual sparring and actually get to what matters. The business executive may fail to recognize that having the largest bank account or the biggest house doesn't necessarily bring fulfillment. The actor may falsely assume that fame is the same thing as happiness. And the social media influencer may equate number of followers with significance.

The Late's ability to be in touch with what is most fashionable also has its flip side. It can lead to a particularly limiting kind of conformity. At the same time that Lates tend to emphasize their individualism, they can fail to connect with what in themselves is in fact individual and uniquely worthy of their attention.

Turning more specifically to Late/Uppers, the other side of the Late/Upper's emphasis on excellence can be a tendency to be overly perfectionistic or self-critical. Late/Uppers can also lose perspective in their obsession with detail and the ideal. And achievement can become a two-edged sword. While the Late/Upper tends to do very well at climbing the ladder of success, he or she can have a difficult time stepping away from it.

Particularly when Capacitance is low, the Late's concern with status can also be a trap. Late/Uppers in particular can find themselves being bigoted and discriminatory on the basis of class. Wealth can end up becoming a person's primary basis for making social distinctions.

We find the most common Late/Upper symptom pattern in the workaholic. Constant activity can be used as a way to feel excitement and to keep doubts at bay—to, in effect, stay high. When life situations challenge the

---

2   See "The Late-Axis Body" later in this chapter, or for more detail and visual depictions, "intelligence's Creative Multiplicity—and a Closer Look at Body Intelligence" in Chapter Nine.

Late/Upper's ascendant posture, the result can be marked anxiety. And when success eludes the Late/Upper, we can sometimes find suicidal degrees of despair. The increasing use of the term "burnout" points toward a growing willingness to examine the partialities of these patterns.

Late/Lower failings are related, but more personal. Excessive outgoingness can translate into feeling distanced from oneself—and paradoxically also from others. And the casual adeptness with surface skills can reduce to trivialness. Breezy can become only superficial; smooth only slick; romantic, seductively manipulative. Oscar Wilde, a Late/Lower who often played humorously with the gifts and blindnesses of Late-Axis sensibility once quipped, "In matters of great importance, style, not sincerity, is the vital thing." It is also the case that competitive spirit can become cattiness and backbiting. I think of the abusive business environment depicted in the movie The Devil Wears Prada. Bette Davis is purported to have once remarked of a fellow actress, "There goes the good time that was had by all."

Late/Lower symptoms tend to reflect the way Lates draw experience from the more surface layers of the emotional. Feelings can easily be disrupted. Late/Lowers may be tormented by self-doubt—particularly in relation to physical appearance (ironic in that it is they who most easily succeed at accepted standards of beauty). It is Late/Lowers, particularly young girls, who tend to be most vulnerable to the traps of modern social media. Late/Lower/Inners especially can become frightened and withdrawn in the face of social pressures. Because of the importance that Late/Lowers put on appearance, eating disorders are especially common with these patterns. For related reasons, older Late/Lowers often have a difficult time with the changes of life's later years.

I've observed that Late-Axis individuals differ more widely in their inclinations than we see with other axes and pointed toward the Creative Function and how we see greatest separation between poles with Late-Axis dynamics. For the same reason, limitations can take widely diverse forms. With

Late/Upper/Outer we can find some of the people who are most rigid in their beliefs; and also, at the extreme of Late/Lower/Inner, people who are as scattered in their sensibilities as the most unformed of Earlies. With regard to culturally mature understanding, at the extreme of Late/Upper/Outer, we find— with certain economists and business executives—some of the most unquestioning of materialist Separation Fallacies. At the extreme of Late/Lower/Inner, we encounter—in advocates of the latest Hollywood diet fad or people who hold some of the oddest of New Age beliefs—some of most irrelevant of Unity Fallacies.

The Late-Axis Body

Late/Uppers tend to carry their bodily charge vertically in the regions of the face and head, and horizontally close to the body surface. Musculature will most often be taut and the body lean. We might commonly use words like stately or statuesque to describe a Late/Upper body. When we see symptoms, both movement and tissue quality will often tend toward the rigid.

With Late/Lower personalities, charge tends similarly to be carried primarily at the body surface, but here it is distributed more evenly. Late/Lower/Outers in particular project more naturally than other temperaments. Where charge is concentrated, it tends to be most in the regions of the face and the pelvis. Because of this, Late/Lowers can sometimes appear to communicate sexual signals even when there is no intent to do so.

Words and Associations

Some phrases given to me from the diverse world of Late-Axis sensibility:

I like to relax by listening to classical music or reading a good book.

I'm by nature pretty articulate.

I was usually quite popular in school. I am still the person who can take a dull party and bring it to life.

I don't like to admit it, but I can be pretty competitive. I like to win.

I feel very at home in the world of ideas.

I make lists. Sometimes I even make lists of lists.

I read a couple of books every month and find great satisfaction in it.

I like to feel classy and put-together. Presentation can make all the difference.

I would make a good television newsperson.

In the end, most of the world's problems are economic.

Your home is not just a place to live, but a statement of who you are.

I like performing. I love the feeling that comes from connecting deeply with an audience.

I can be a bit excitable. People say they like this in me. They think I'm a fun person.

Luxuriating in a tub with fine bath oil and a glass of wine is a perfect way to end my day.

I like things in my life to be clean and well-organized.

I feel at home in the quick pace and culture of cities like New York, Paris, or Hong Kong.

When I need a pick-me-up, I get my hair done or go shopping for something fun.

My friends tend to be well-read—insightful people with keen minds.

Romance is happiness.

I value the finer things in life.

Lates and the Future

Because Lates tend to identity with achievement and advancement, they often give more day-to-day attention to the future than other temperaments. And many futurists, particularly of the business and government sort, are Lates. When Lates begin to engage Cultural Maturity's changes, in potential they bring particular sophistication to articulating what makes those changes important.

But characteristics common to Late-Axis personalities can also easily get in the way when it comes to culturally mature understanding. The focus of Late thinkers tends to be the short-term—the next business, election, or news cycle. And the Late's native cognitive makeup can make it difficult for them to recognize the importance of culturally mature understanding, and thus to effectively realize it. Lates are likely to assume that Modern Age thought, with its rationalist, materialist underpinnings, is an ideal and end point and to define advancement in terms of new technologies and economic growth. And when it comes to institutional structures, Lates tend to think in terms of protecting and further refining existing forms to adapt to the changes of technological progress.

These limitations can have major significance. I think, for example, of the fact that Lates make most decisions in higher education. I see this as a major contributor to the fact that today's academic world provides less leadership than we might hope when it comes to culturally mature understanding. And the fact that Lates largely control serious journalism means that the world of information confronts a related predicament.[3]

---

[3] The great majority of content in The New York Times, for example, is written by Lates.

A Late-Axis Vignette

One of my favorite personal Late-Axis vignettes comes from years back when I lead an ongoing think tank on the future of public media at my local public television station. In Chapter Seven, I'll return for some reflections on how I structured the think tank and the way it drew on people with diverse temperaments in order to be most effective. With this chapter, I will turn instead to my relationship with a person in the group who over time became not just a valued colleague, but a friend. He is a Late, then a top executive at the station. Besides the time we spent together in think tank sessions, we made a habit of periodically getting together for lunch.

It is rare that I wear a tie when I work. This is in part because I am an Early; in part, because of the kinds of setting where I tend to spend my time. The public television think tank was one of the exceptions. Because of the professional nature of the context and my particular role, a tie seemed appropriate. But as you might imagine, I don't have a large selection of ties in my closet to choose from.

Once when we were talking over lunch, my Late-Axis friend and colleague casually observed that I had only three ties. I had never thought about how many ties I had, and I am quite sure that he had not thought about it that much either. Rather, simply, it was something he noticed. Over the years I rotated through those that I owned and he recognized this fact.

I often think back to that lunch when reflecting on personality style differences. There is much in life that I notice that he never would, but I can't even begin to imagine noticing something like a colleague's tie supply. And certainly I can't imagine doing so without effort, as was clearly the case for him. It was an important personality-style aha moment. I was confronted in a particularly inescapable way with how, while I might have much in common with another person and even be friends, in terms of temperament, we could almost come from different planets.

CHAPTER FIVE

Overarching Observations

I've pointed toward a variety of ways that we need to expand understanding if we are to make full use of the Creative Systems Theory Personality Typology. After reflecting briefly on the typology's beginnings, here we will look in more detail at several of them. I will probe a bit deeper into the kinds of complexities and common confusions that I began to address in Chapter One. I will bring a finer lens to the various types of distinctions that the theory draws on and how they work together to paint a larger picture. We will look more deeply at the concept of Creative Symptoms and how it relates to temperament. I will then tie temperament more closely to the concept of Cultural Maturity by filling out observations about the kinds of systemic traps and fallacies to which each Axis is most vulnerable. I will briefly address the question of etiology, how we end up with temperament differences in the first place. I will touch on how these notions relate to other kinds of difference such as gender and ethnic background. And I'll conclude by reflecting on ways that the typology can help us better make our way in today's changing relationship realities, and by affirming the roles that people of all temperaments can play in the kind of understanding the future will increasingly require.

The Typology's Origins

A person may at first find the relationship between creative stages and personality styles that underlies the typology surprising. On first encounter it surprised me. It is a recognition original to Creative Systems Theory. And it has unexpected consequences beyond its practical implications. If accurate, it provides powerful support for the theory's claim that a creative frame provides a fundamental step forward in how we understand.

Years back, it was where the Creative Systems Personality Typology, in fact, had its beginnings. When in college, I took a series of quite amazing classes on world music.[4] We were introduced each day to music from far-flung places, music that we had never heard before. As I listened, I was struck by the contrasting ways different people in the room often reacted to music from various periods in culture. Certain people, on experiencing a particular kind of music, would respond with immediate identification. In spite of the fact that the music was wholly new to them, somehow it was saying "Come home to Mama." For other people, the reaction might be almost the opposite. At the extreme, they would respond with aversion, as if the music was fingernails on a blackboard. A few days later, with music from a different period in culture's evolution, the reactions might be just the opposite. The "Come home to Mama" group might now respond as if what they were hearing was fingernails on a blackboard, and the other group the reverse.

While I didn't yet have the CSPT to draw on, over time I began to recognize patterns in these responses. It appeared that people who had similar personalities were reacting in related ways to music from particular times in culture. Later, with the beginning insights of Creative Systems Theory, these early observations began to make more sense. I saw that specific personality styles, like cultural stages, drew preferentially on particular intelligences and kinds of cognitive organization. The Creative Systems Personality Typology grew out of these further reflections.

---

4   Taught by Dr. Robert Garfias at the University of Washington.

More Complexities and Common Confusions

For ease of communication, I've made temperament distinctions largely as if there were twelve relatively discrete personality categories. But I've also emphasized the importance of appreciating nuance. For example, I've described how Early-, Middle-, and Late-Axis dynamics are not just separate categories, but lie along a continuum. Similarly, we are always dealing with interplays between Upper and Lower poles, Inner and Outer aspects. We must be ready for such subtleties if the typology is to be most useful.

Identifying a few figures whose personality styles situate midway between axes helps clarify how we are dealing with continua rather than discrete categories. People whose temperaments reside at the cusp between Early and Middle include Mark Twain, Whoopi Goldberg, Bessie Smith, and W. C. Fields. A few from the cusp between Middle and Late include Franklin Roosevelt, Princess Diana, Sean Connery, and Arthur Ashe. "Bimodal" patterns, where a personality structure has dual points of emphasis, are less common than people tend to assume, but we do find them on occasion. They can happen, for example, when a person with an Early-Axis personality is born into a Late-Axis family, or where there is a major cultural influence, as with a Late-Axis individual with strong Middle or Early-Axis cultural roots.

We can expand on these observations by highlighting how familiar figures from particular cultural spheres situate along temperament continua. Political leadership provides a good example. Most political leaders have Upper/Outer personalities centered about mid-way between Middle-Axis and Late-Axis. They need both the Middle's capacity to manage people and Late's skills with detail, abstraction, and appearance to be successful. We find a continuum, ranging from John Kennedy or Barack Obama toward Late, to Jessie Helms and Ted Cruz on the far Middle-Axis end of the spectrum. Bill Clinton had more lower than most politicians (Middle with a touch of Late).[5] George W. Bush had a similar balance vertically, but with more Middle, and somewhat lower Capacitance. Joe Biden's temperament is mostly Late/Upper/Inner, but with a touch of Middle as we see with his ability to engage blue collar values.[6]

We can use the physical appeal of familiar Hollywood personalities to illustrate styles along the continuum between Middle/Lower and Late/Lower. Looking first to women, the attractiveness of a Julia Roberts, Halle Berry, or Michelle Pfeiffer is pretty purely Late/Lower. Each exudes an easy, refined sensuality. Madonna's temperament, while largely Late/Lower, also has a distinct Middle/Lower edge. We are never too far from the rebel and a certain need to shock. Mae West and Dolly Parton take us a bit over the line into Middle/Lower. (I've observed how Taylor Swift and Lisa Kudrow are Earlies.) On the male side, the appeal of a Robert Redford, Sidney Poitier, or Clark Gable exemplify nearly pure Late/Lower male sexuality—the romantic ideal. With Tom Cruise or Richard Gere we get a touch of Middle; with Tom Selleck or Harrison Ford a bit more; and with Burt Reynolds, Arnold Schwarzenegger, or Clint Eastwood we move fully over the line into Middle. (I've noted how Marlon Brando and Jack Nicholson are each Earlies).

Certain commonly-found temperament dynamics can initially cause confusion and warrant a closer look. In one—what CST calls "cross-polar" patterns—the pole a person identifies with and the pole that they most speak from are not the same. We find a common cross-polar dynamic in the self-righteous victim who identifies with being oppressed while at the same time criticizing from a position of "on-high" superiority. We encounter this particular example most frequently with Middles, but we can see it with any

---

5   Remember his propensity for Big Macs, his saxophone, and his comfort in talking with the "common folk" in town meetings.

6   I think of Donald Trump as something of a special case. He has more Late/Outer than previous presidents and also lower Capacitance than most, along with more explicit Symptom patterns.

temperament axis. With Lates, we often encounter cross-polar dynamics where there is identification with the archetypally feminine in the context of Late-Axis's more strongly archetypally masculine reality. Late-Axis academic thought that identifies with left-hand sensibilities can manifest as a highly intellectual anti-intellectualism. (The worst of postmodern thought gets caught in this sort of contradiction.) Late-Axis cross-polar patterns are also common with the more populist of progressive political beliefs. At the extreme, Upper Pole authority can reduce to a posture that is, in effect, anti-authoritarian.

Similarities between certain very different personality types can cause particular confusion. One example involves two temperaments commonly found in academia. The majority of professors have Late/Upper/Inner personalities. But we also find a fair number of Early/Upper/Outers. If an Early-Axis person's temperament is highly Upper Pole, he or she can be just as comfortable with the intellect and just as much identify with objective inquiry. There are useful clues for teasing them apart. For example, the Earlies tend to have a harder time keeping their hair combed and are frequently difficult to find beneath the "ecological complexity" of their offices. They are also less naturally comfortable with the structures of academic life. But we must go beyond behavior to the underlying temperament dynamic to really make the distinction.

We find a second easily confusing distinction with people of more artistic inclination. Artistic interests manifest most strongly with two temperaments that on the surface could hardly be more different: Earlies (more Early/Outers with the expressive arts) and Late/Lower/Inners. Dancers and visual artists can come from either. We get a few temperament clues from looking at the form of the person's creative expression. In dance, Earlies often most enjoy improvisation, while Lates are likely to prefer dance that is more choreographed. In painting, the Early artist is more apt to work abstractly, the Late artist more representationally.

A simple insight makes what we see with each of these easily confusing juxtapositions more understandable. While Early/Outer and Late/Inner reflect widely different dynamics, the balance between more form-defined (more archetypically masculine) and more creatively germinal (archetypically feminine) within each is very similar. Early/Outer represents the most form-defined pattern within the least form-defined axis. And Late/Inner represents the least form-defined pattern within the most form-defined axis. It is not surprising, then, at least at first blush, that these styles can appear quite similar.

A more general kind of common confusion follows from an overarching characteristic of temperament complexity. While each axis most reflects the reality of a single creative stage, within the reality of that axis we also find sensibilities that mirror the whole of creative organization. It can be easy to assume that we find all the diversity we need within our own slice of things. At the extreme, a Late-Axis personality with strong Lower/Inner leanings could be more concerned with creative beginnings than the average Early. And an Early that was biased strongly toward Upper/Outer could be more concerned with appearances and refinement than the average Late. This diversity within each Axis plays a major role in why we have tended not to recognize temperament differences.

Distinctions and their Interplay

In Chapter One, I observed that applying temperament concepts most precisely and powerfully requires that we draw on all of the various kinds of patterning distinctions that I then touched on. It is an observation that warrants going a bit beyond what I have described. Here is a brief summary of the systemic variables that I have thus far noted:

- *The defining axis (Early, Middle, or Late)—the place in formative process as a whole that a person preferentially embodies as a function of his or her unique temperament.*

- *Vertical and Horizontal contributions—pole, and aspect variables.*
- *A person's overall Capacitance.*
- *The kinds of Symptoms a person will be most predisposed to, given all of the above.*
- *A person's capacity for culturally mature perspective (directly related to Capacitance).*
- *Where a person resides in the various developmental/creative processes that order their temporal existence (lifetime most strongly, but also cultural stage and stage in other important creative processes such as profession and family)*

All of these variables are pertinent and can at times be particularly important to consider. It may be enough to note that a person's temperament is primarily Middle-Axis. But, as we've seen, a person who is more Middle/Outer will view the world very differently from a person who is more Middle/Inner. Pole and aspect observations can sometimes be more striking and of greater consequence when making comparisons than those that focus on temperament axis.

The same can be true with Capacitance. A person who has the requisite temperament for a certain kind of contribution may nonetheless lack the Capacitance needed to succeed with that contribution or to function effectively in the relationships it requires. And the way Capacitance ties to other variables adds to the significance. Capacitance differences will determine if we see Symptoms. And when our interest lies with collaboration in addressing critical cultural issues, the most important variable may be a person's capacity for culturally mature perspective.

Patterning in Time variables can also intersect with temperament in ways that need to be forefront in our considerations. Certainly this is the case with personal development. Early-, Middle-, or Late-Axis temperament attributes are going to manifest very differently in a person who is ten years old versus someone who is forty. And often we need to be particularly attentive to differences that are products of cultural stage. The same personality style will express itself in characteristically different ways depending on when in culture's evolutionary story the person lives.

Besides personality style, Creative Systems Theory also makes other sorts of Patterning in Space distinctions. For example, the theory describes how cultural domains can be understood in terms of here-and-now systemic patterns. I've pointed toward this relationship in noting how professions tend to be associated with particular temperaments—the arts with Early-Axis, education with Middle-Axis, business with Late-Axis, and so on. We can also apply Patterning in Space distinctions to help us understand beliefs and aesthetic preferences within specific cultural spheres. They can help us better understand not just why different people may reach different conclusions, but also the particular contributions—and particular blindnesses—that accompany different conclusions. In Chapter Seven, I will draw on this kind of discernment to examine how temperament correlates with Patterning in Space–related variables such as political ideology, religious belief, preferences in music, sports and recreational activities one might participate in, and clothing styles.

One application of this sort of observation proves particularly helpful when attempting to bring systemic perspective to understanding within a particular cultural domain or academic discipline. A close look reveals that the contrasting beliefs of differing schools of thought in any sphere will tend to mirror the personality style biases of the school's originator. As illustration, in my field of psychiatry Carl Jung was an Early/Upper/Inner, Sigmund Freud a Middle/Upper, and B. F. Skinner a Late/Upper/Inner. These men's contributions to modern psychology each directly reflect what we would expect from their temperament's place within a larger systemic picture.

Creative Symptoms

In Chapter One, I introduced the concept of Creative Symptoms. And with each of the three axis-specific chapters, I've noted Symptom patterns that we commonly find with each temperament. The notion warrants a closer look. Besides providing essential nuance when addressing temperament, the concept of Creative Symptoms offers important insight with regard to how the Creative Systems Personality Typology takes us beyond common thinking about human limitations and challenges.

The relationship between Capacitance and Creative Symptoms makes a good place to start. The theory describes how human systems perceive challenging experiences as meaningful—"true," in a creative sense—up to the limits of their Capacitance. At that point they become unsettled—perturbation ensues. We have common language for ways individuals may respond symptomatically when they lack the Capacitance a situation requires. We talk of people "losing it," becoming "reactive," or getting "bent out of shape."

"Symptom" is not an ideal term. As commonly used, the word implies only pathology. As I will get to shortly, the significance is more interesting than just this. But because the link between Symptoms in this specifically systemic sense and other dynamics with which we commonly associate the word is strong, I've chosen to use it. Better understanding mechanisms that may underlie symptoms in the word's more conventional usage is one of the most important implications of the way that Creative Systems Theory applies the term.

While Creative Symptoms take a great multiplicity of forms, the underlying strategy with each is the same. We retreat into identification with isolated aspects of our complexity. Symptoms are unconscious, psychological, protective mechanisms that work by exaggerating common vertical and horizontal psychological tendencies. Some polar diversions shield us by lifting us above the perceived threat (e.g., intellectualization or grandiosity), while others drop us below the potential insult (e.g., depression or the victim posture of passive aggression). Some shift our attention internal to the threat (e.g., withdrawal or denial), while others direct our focus external to the threat (e.g., combativeness or obsessively busying ourselves).

Note that each kind of Symptom exists on a continuum with everyday responses. Each reflects an exaggerated expression of a polar tendency. At one extreme, rigor becomes rigor mortis. At the opposite extreme, flexibility becomes a lifeless puddle.

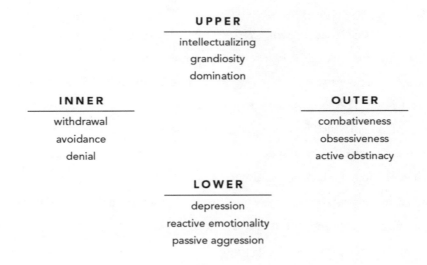

Fig. 5-1. A Sampling of Vertical and Horizontal Psychological Symptoms

We can combine these general observations with descriptions from the previous three chapters about the particular forms that Creative Symptoms commonly take with each temperament axis. The result is a detailed picture of how Symptoms are most likely to manifest which helps us appreciate just how and why they do.

I've noted that the concept of Creative Symptoms helps take us beyond common thinking about limitations and challenges. In Chapter Nine, I will tie the concept more directly to common notions of psychopathology. A key recognition is that thinking of Creative Symptoms only as problems misses important aspects of their significance. In each case, what we see can be understood as, at once, evidence of limitation and a description of creatively important protective mechanisms.

When a system reaches the limits of its Capacitance, it will do one of three things: It will expand itself and grows; it will act consciously to protect itself (so the creative vessel will not be extended too far); or it will protect itself covertly—hopefully with enough effectiveness that major damage is avoided. Symptom, as CST uses the word, reflects this third kind of option.

We tend to think of the first response as most ideal, and in a sense it is. But growing in response works only if we have close to the needed Capacitance in the first place. The second approach—the conscious making of boundaries—offers safety while also leaving options available. However, this approach can also require significant Capacitance—and often at just the time when Capacitance may be lacking. And while conscious boundaries let us be more nuanced in our responses, they can also put us further at risk. They make a system more visible and thus a more obvious target.

Because Symptoms tend be unconscious, they provide a particularly impenetrable kind of boundary and an effective last line of defense. The problem with Symptoms is that we also pay a high price for this added safety. Symptoms diminish flexibility—they are reactive and often habitual. They also distort reality. And they block not just experience that threatens to harm, but also that which we need in order to learn and adapt. When chronic, Symptoms can slow or even arrest development. But the price can be very much worth it if significant harm would result from the breaching of boundaries.

Polar Fallacies

I promised to return for a closer look at a related kind of concept I often use when addressing the specific challenges presented by Cultural Maturity's changes. The terms Separation Fallacy, Unity Fallacy, and Compromise Fallacy refer to three basic ways we can fail when attempting to think more systemically. Polar fallacies function like Symptoms, but in relation to the specific tasks of Cultural Maturity. This basic fallacy framework served as the foundation for my 1991 book, Necessary Wisdom. There I used it to tease apart common conceptual blindnesses found with concerns as diverse as leadership, love, morality, medicine, science, religion, and global relations.[7]

Sometimes, falling for a polar fallacy is a consequence only of momentary misunderstanding. But more often it reflects an underlying psychological/cognitive pattern. If we are vulnerable to polar fallacies, we are likely to fall for the same general sort of trap whatever the question we consider. Particularly important for this book's reflections, people with different personality styles are going to be most vulnerable to particular kinds of polar fallacies.

I often use the image of a doorway to clarify how the kind of "bridging" of polarities that characterizes culturally mature systemic understanding is wholly different from averaging or compromise. Integrative Meta-perspective, rather than joining the two sides of the archway, is represented by going through the archway and into the territory beyond. Expanding on this image highlights the particular ways that these three kinds of polar fallacies miss the mark, and also how they relate to each other.

---

[7] Charles M. Johnston, MD, Necessary Wisdom: Meeting the Challenge of a New Cultural Maturity, 1991, Celestial Arts.

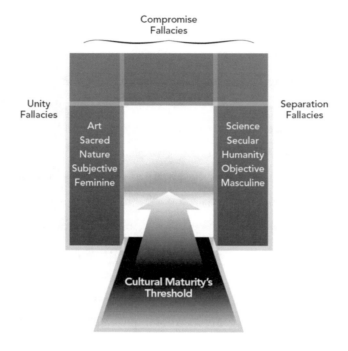

Fig. 5-2. Polar Fallacies and Cultural Maturity

Unity Fallacies fall off the left side of Cultural Maturity's threshold. They identify with the archetypally feminine. Unity Fallacies might include: In the end, we are all one (differences are ultimately irrelevant). The ordinary person knows best (better than leaders and institutions). Final truth is what we know from within. The task is to always live in accord with nature. Everything happens for a reason, even if that reason remains mysterious (it is all connected).

Unity Fallacies argue against distinction and emphasize oneness. They may claim a transcendence of polarity, but in fact they very specifically take sides. They give their allegiance to the softer, more creatively germinal hand of creation—to the spiritual over the material, feelings over facts, the timeless over the specific. We find Unity Fallacies with romantic, liberal/humanist, philosophically idealist, extreme environmentalist, and New Age views.

Separation Fallacies fall off the right side of Cultural Maturity's threshold. They identify with the archetypally masculine. In doing so they equate truth with difference—with perceived fundamental distinctions such as those between men and women, the material and the spiritual, or the intellect and the emotions. They also give greatest value to the more creatively manifest side of the pertinent polarity (here men, the material, and the intellect). Some related Separation Fallacies include: We are each wholly unique, individual. Experts have the answers. Final truth is what can be rationally articulated and objectively demonstrated. Humanity is wholly separate from nature and has rightful dominion over it. Change is a simple product of cause and effect.

We see Separation Fallacies suggested with positivist and behaviorist views, and also with ideas that reduce to a narrow scientism. We also encounter Separation Fallacies with technological gospel beliefs that make invention the assumed answer to future problems, and with extreme materialist economic models that idealize unfettered free markets. Another place we encounter Separation Fallacies is with conservative political views that emphasize differences—"Build that wall."

Compromise Fallacies split the difference. A few related Compromise Fallacies are: We are all different in our own ways ("different strokes for different folks"). Good decisions come from everybody having their particular say. There are lots of kinds of truth, and each has its merits. Nature can be different things to different people. In the end, life is what we make of it.

Some Compromise Fallacies advocate a safe, additive middle ground. Others argue correctly for multiple options, but give us nothing to help us beyond this accurate but meager observation— they claim to address diversity but fail to address what makes differences different. Compromise Fallacies take us beyond black and white, but in the end provide instead only shades of gray.

Compromise Fallacies manifest most explicitly with postmodern interpretations. But we also see them any time a person takes a polarity—content and process, masculine and feminine, or mind and body—and observes simply that both sides are true without also articulating just how this might be the case, and at least a bit about where getting beyond polarity takes us.[8]

Temperament helps fill out the concept of Polar Fallacy. I've observed that Earlies can be particularly vulnerable to Unity Fallacies and Lates to Separation Fallacies. We can also add further detail. Each type of fallacy has many versions, some of which are more common with certain personality styles, some with others.

For example, we can talk of multiple, very different kinds of Unity Fallacies. We encounter an intellectual sort of Unity Fallacy with academic and liberal (Late-Axis) thought that sides with the underprivileged and polarizes against conservatives and corporations. We confront a more ardent variety of Unity Fallacy with fundamentalist religious (Middle-Axis) beliefs that ally with "family values" and polarize against intellectual elites. And we find Unity Fallacies of a more specifically spiritual sort with advocates of New Age or back-to-the-land (Early-Axis) philosophies.

Similarly, we can talk of a variety of kinds of Separation Fallacies. While the Late's more intellectual or business-related Separation Fallacies may be most obvious, we find Separation Fallacies of a particularly intractable sort in the moral absolutism that often accompanies Middle-Axis sensibilities. And while the techno-utopian beliefs common with Earlies can seem almost

---

[8] Polar fallacies of any of these three types represent shorthand concepts. As a start, no one type of fallacy is as distinct from the others as the labels might suggest. If you look closely, you will see, for example, that Unity Fallacies commonly carry a hidden Separation Fallacy, and that Separation Fallacies similarly often carry a hidden Unity Fallacy. A person who sees his own group as "chosen" and a conflicting group as "evil" succumbs to a Unity Fallacy with regard to his compatriots and a Separation Fallacy in relation to his adversaries.

spiritually inspired, in having their basis in a loss of connectedness with bodily experience, they reflect a rather ultimate sort of Separation Fallacy.

Compromise Fallacies can similarly manifest with any axis. With Late-Axis we can find them with both liberal and postmodern beliefs. The Middle/Inner's desire to have people get along can result in Compromise Fallacy conclusions. And an Early-Axis identification with unity can also often in practice translate into Compromise Fallacy.

As with an appreciation for the underlying dynamics of Symptoms, we can learn a lot from Polar Fallacies and their workings. Such understanding can help us recognize limits to Capacitance and ways in which we may protect ourselves from life's very real complexities and uncertainties. It can also help us make sense of where growth may be needed, in this case with regard to today's essential challenges at a species level.

Etiology and Personality Style

Given how great personality style differences can be, it is reasonable to wonder why particular individuals have the personality characteristics that they do. Perhaps surprisingly, Creative Systems Theory, by itself, doesn't provide a definitive answer. But observations that come from using the typology do point us in useful directions.

The evidence suggests that, while learning plays at least some role, in most instances genetic mechanisms have the greater influence. I've noted how bimodal patterns can occur when a person's context during development differs greatly from their native personality style. This suggests some role for nurture as well as nature. But the contribution of conditioning in general appears less than we might imagine. For example, when first developing the typology, I wondered how applicable it would be to children. It turns out that temperament differences are often most obvious with very young children.[9] This is what we would predict if nature as apposed to nurture were the stronger influence. We find further evidence in family structure. While most children have personality styles similar to their parents, with high frequency we also find striking differences. Both nature and nurture would be expected to produce similarities. But genetic mechanisms are also consistent with significant variation.

We also find a more conceptual kind of evidence for the role of nature as opposed to nurture. The idea that temperament is a product of cognition's creative organization supports a genetic explanation. At least the underlying structures that temperament differences draw on clearly have genetic roots.

Other factors may also contribute. For example, some kind of "ecological niche" dynamic likely plays at least a minor role. Multiple children in a family tend to disperse within the personality spectrum—most likely as a way to provide distinct territory for each child's identity.

Gender

A question people often ask in getting started is whether we see gender-related differences with the typology. The broader topic of gender differences today can become volatile. There are people who argue that there exist no innate psychological differences between men and women, that any differences we might imagine are products only of cultural conditioning. These days, a person can lose their job in academia by suggesting otherwise.

---

9 In Chapter Eight, I will include some specific reflections on temperament and children from teachers who have worked to apply the typology in school settings. These further observations will help bring nuance to our understanding of how temperament differences manifest at different ages. They will also illustrate how to apply such understanding with the best of teaching.

Creative Systems Theory Patterning in Time notions provide perspective for understanding today's changing gender realities.[10] The theory describes how most past ideas about gender have been based on projection. Historically, men have projected more archetypally feminine parts of their cognitive complexity onto women and women have projected the more archetypally masculine parts of their cognitive complexity on men. With Cultural Maturity this changes. Integrative Meta-perspective makes it newly possible to own such projection and to more fully acknowledge the complexity that exists within each of us.

This picture very much supports the importance of getting beyond past gender stereotypes. But it also challenges the assumption that the result is only some postmodern unisex reality. Culturally mature perspective helps us recognize how there are more similarities than differences between men and women—and marked exceptions to the patterns we do see. But it also offers that we might better appreciate actual differences.

I find one such difference-related generalization particularly useful, and also helpful for thinking about temperament. When we step beyond projective dynamics, we tend to find about a 60/40 balance of archetypal qualities relative to gender. Men on average (there are major exceptions) embody a bit more of the archetypally masculine; women a bit more of the archetypally feminine. This basic pattern is reflected in personality style differences. We find about equal numbers of men and women in each axis. But we also see on average about a 60/40 balance relative to gender between the more form-defined and less form-defined poles—men with a greater leaning toward Upper Pole and Outer Aspect, women toward Lower Pole and Inner Aspect. The observation is consistent with how I have spoken of Upper Pole and Outer Aspect

---

10   See Charles M. Johnston, MD, On the Evolution of Intimacy: A Brief Exploration into the Past, Present, and Future of Gender and Love, 2019, ICD Press.

personalities as leaning toward the archetypally masculine and Lower Pole and Inner Aspect personalities as leaning towards the archetypally feminine.

Again, the question of etiology is not formally answered. But we can say with some certainty that something beyond mere conditioning is at work. A woman's body tends to remain softer to the touch than that of a man even with the same amount of exercise (consistent with a greater natural tendency toward Inner Aspects). With this, men tend to carry their center of balance on average about two inches higher than women of the same height (consistent with a greater natural tendency toward Upper Pole dynamics). Integrative Meta-perspective "bridges" masculine and feminine, making us all "non-binary." But it also "bridges" mind and body, making each of us more connected with ourselves as gendered beings.

We can make some beginning generalizations with regard to people with other than heterosexual leanings and traditional gender identification, but observations are purely empirical. In my experience as a therapist, in the personalities of gay men, more often than we might otherwise expect, we find Late-Axis dynamics, particularly Late/Lower and Late/Inner, with additional smaller groupings in Middle-Axis and Early-Axis. Middle-Axis dynamics seem to be more common than we would otherwise expect among women who identify as lesbian, though there are many exceptions. The larger portion of people I have met who identify as transgender are Earlies or Middle/Lowers.

Race, Ethnicity, and Locale

The question of variation between cultural groups can be even more controversial. Differences described historically have tended to be based on the projections of bigotry and racism. Culturally mature perspective helps us get beyond such projection. But at the same time, it again opens the door to appreciating real differences. It turns out that people of various cultural backgrounds can differ normatively not just in terms of cultural mores and assumptions, but also with regard to the balance of personality styles within their populations.

For example, in my experience, among people of equal Capacitance residing in the U.S., we find a somewhat higher percentage than average of Early/Lower and Middle/Lower personalities in Native American, South Sea Islander, Hispanic, and African American populations; of Early/Upper/Inner and Middle/Upper/Inner personalities in Americans of Asian background; of Middle-Axis personalities (both Upper and Lower) in Americans of Eastern European, Scandinavian, Germanic and Irish extraction; and of Late-Axis personalities in Americans of predominantly English, French, or Italian heritage (with English more Late/Upper, French more Late/Lower, and Italian midway between Middle-Axis and Late/Lower). The explanation likely involves a combination of Patterning in Time and Patterning in Space variables.

The differences are in most cases small, but they can have significant implications. For example, traditional public education does very poorly at addressing the needs of Early/Lower and Middle/Lower kids—whatever their backgrounds. The aspects of intelligence where these personality styles on average most excel are largely ignored. Not surprisingly, youth from cultural groups where these personalities styles occur with higher than average frequency tend more often than others to feel estranged in public education and to thrive less well in traditional educational contexts than one might hope and expect. This observation suggests that, while increasing the amount of educational content that relates to the specific experiences of different groups has an important place in educational reform, making education more responsive to our multiple intelligences and to the unique realities of different personality styles may be as or more important in the long run.

Looking to the Future Through the Lens of Relationship

A good way to tie the typology to the challenges of Cultural Maturity is to look at how it assists us with new interpersonal realities. Along with helping us understand individual identity with new sophistication, the typology also serves us in important ways when it comes to how we engage with others. It helps us better understand why we might see one another and react to each other in the particular ways that we do. It also provides immediate guidance for the tasks of collaboration.

Love Relationships

If the concept of Cultural Maturity is accurate, better appreciating temperament differences should become increasingly important in the world of love. Until recently, people have tended to date and marry individuals who had similar personality styles. We often say opposites attract, but this has generally been opposites from within one's own temperament axis. Today, people are more often having relationships where the other person may have a wholly different personality style.

Such cross-type attraction is most common when individuals are beginning to live their lives as a whole in culturally mature ways. Cultural Maturity's changes make it newly possible to base love not just on romantic projection, but on the actual experience of another whole person.[11] If love's attraction comes ultimately from our ability to make each other's lives more, and "more" today increasingly means the ability to hold the whole of systemic complexity, then we would expect differences that before might have produced only confusion and conflict to now become newly attractive.

---

[11] Again, see *On the Evolution of Intimacy*.

Adding temperament diversity to love's equation doesn't at all make love easier. Bringing culturally mature perspective to love is, by itself, demanding enough. Love becomes even more demanding when the other person, along with inhabiting his or her own particular uniqueness, also lives in a world of experience that even with the best of efforts we can never understand as fully as our own. But this additional ingredient can, in a further timely and significant sense, make partners in love potential "teachers" to one another.

Group Affiliations

Group associations—in churches, community organizations, and with political/social advocacy—have historically often lacked diversity when it comes to temperament. But just as today we are seeing greater gender and racial diversity in such contexts, in the future we should also find greater temperament diversity, particularly with organizations that have high Capacitance. Knowledge of temperament differences and skills at communication between temperaments should have growing importance in group settings of all sorts. Businesses, at least of any size, have for practical reasons

often been more diverse in this respect. I've used the fact that businesses rely on an array of temperaments to carry out different creative functions—Early's for more R&D, Middles for manufacturing and management, Lates for finance and marketing—to introduce the typology. But in times past, these various functions have been kept relatively separate. The more global, fast-paced businesses of the future will need to be more dynamically integrated to function effectively, something we are beginning to see. These changes will require greater sophistication with regard to both how we view our own temperaments and how we relate to people with temperaments different from our own.

Temperament and the Future of Leadership

Leadership, whatever the sphere, has in times past been almost exclusively a Middle/Upper or Late/Upper cultural function. And leadership relationships have been largely polar "top-down" leader/follower relationships. The concept of Cultural Maturity predicts three kinds of changes in times ahead that are pertinent to the topic of temperament, each of which we are beginning to see. We should find people of other temperaments more often taking on leadership roles. We should see those being led having an increasingly empowered role in the leadership relationship. And we should more and more appreciate how decisions that involve diverse creative input are likely to be most effective.

This more systemic picture means that leaders of organizations need to be more knowledgeable about temperament differences and more adept in working with groups that include temperament diversity. It also means that all people involved in collective decision-making processes (and, in a world of more participatory leadership that means everyone) need the sophistication of communications skills that can come only with a deep understanding of personality differences.

With nation state and global leadership, I've given greatest attention in my writing to the importance of taking Pattering in Time differences into account. Effective leadership requires an appreciation of how different people's assumptions can be at various points in culture's evolving story. But effective decision-making on the global stage will also require greater comfort with temperament diversity and a greater ability to work in its presence.

One example stands out in these divisive times: It follows from the concept of Cultural Maturity that neither traditionally liberal nor traditionally conservative political positions will be sufficient for addressing the questions before us. In Chapter Seven, I will touch on how we can tie the beliefs of the political left and the political right to the worldviews of particular temperaments and their accompanying creative partialities. The importance of getting beyond partisan bickering and finding the ability to achieve truly creative solutions is another place where better understanding personality style differences should prove important.

In the Introduction, I noted a more encompassing kind of significance when describing my work with think tank groups. To use the box-of-crayons metaphor, personality differences provide the various, creatively-related hues needed if we are to successfully address the important questions ahead for us as a species and have a positive human future. I've emphasized that no personality style has a leg up when it comes to culturally mature capacities. I've also noted how all temperaments in potential have significant roles to play in a culturally mature world. If you want effective culturally mature decision-making, put together a high Capacitance team that includes solid representatives from each axis.

CHAPTER SIX

Vignettes

Simple stories provide one of the best ways for an appreciation of temperament differences to begin to feel like common sense. After starting with a vignette that reflects back on the origins of Creative Systems Theory, I will follow with a few that fall into basic categories: identity vignettes, comparative vignettes, relationship vignettes, organizational vignettes, and developmental vignettes.

Writing My First Book

The importance of taking personality style into account confronted me in a dramatic and unexpected way with the writing of my first book, The Creative Imperative. By that time I had a basic understanding of how notions like Early-Axis, Middle-Axis, and Late-Axis applied not just to change, but also to temperament. And it was clear to me that each kind of sensibility was creative, and in the end, equally so. But, like everyone, I have a particular personality style. Much more so than I at first understood, this would affect my efforts in getting started.

I was not happy when I first recognized this intrusion. More and more often as I wrote, I encountered situations that required that I question my Early-Axis assumptions. And, ultimately, work with the book would challenge me even more deeply. I had to face that what I was trying to do would demand more than just some enlarging of the lens I was applying, being more inclusive in my considerations. I was beginning to grasp how Creative Systems Theory reflected a new kind of understanding, how it required that we fundamentally rethink how we think. Recognizing basic ways that my temperament—and any temperament—was necessarily partial demanded in a whole new sense that I appreciate how deeply this was the case.[1]

This kind of realization would make itself felt in a very immediate—and personal—way. A year into work on the book, I gathered the pages I had written and placed them in the fireplace. To get beyond my Early-Axis bias, it would not be enough to simply revise and edit what I had written. Ways of thinking that stopped short of what Creative Systems Theory is ultimately about were embedded in every sentence. I had been very happy with much that I had written. Indeed, it had seemed to me quite inspiring. But if I was to honor what gave the book a reason to be written in the first place, I would need to again start from scratch.

It has been said that good writing and thinking requires that we be willing to "murder our darlings"—and particularly those we find most beautiful. In the development of Creative Systems Theory, this was one of my most important "murdering my darlings" moments. It was possible only because I had become familiar with the basic contours of the theory's temperament framework and had at least a beginning appreciation for the depths at which temperament differences are different and important.

Identity and Perception Vignettes

The following three vignettes come from Intensive (year-long) trainings at the Institute for Creative Development. Each highlights gifts and blindnesses we find with particular temperaments. Each also sheds light on how those gifts and blindnesses can appear to people of other personality styles.

---

1 Earlier I used the metaphor of a box of crayons. The task is more than just including all the crayons, though that is a start. We need to think from the encompassing box's more fully systemic vantage.

An Early-Axis Vignette: "Lates treat Earlies like pets."

A participant in one of my trainings was a tall, gangly man who was widely appreciated in the Seattle art scene for his skills as a performance artist. His aesthetic style was extremely physical. Often he used no words at all; his movements were all that was needed. I remember someone once asking him his favorite animal. Before our eyes he literally became a praying mantis. He was quite obviously an Early/Lower.

In Chapter Seven, I will describe an exercise that I've often used in trainings once people are generally familiar with the typology. I first divide people up by axis and have people in each small group examine what they have in common. I then bring the large group back together and invite each axis group, in turn, to make a presentation about their experience together. I then invite the other two groups to ask curiosity questions.

When the Earlies made their presentation, someone asked the performance artist what it was like to have such an unusual profession. He responded that he had an easier time than many Early artists because there was a ready audience for his work. In those times, Earlies too often ended up being "starving artists."

A brief discussion followed about the fact that, while most artists are Earlies, many of the people who most support the arts are Lates. Someone asked him how we felt about that fact. There was a significant, somewhat awkward pause. He then responded that he had no problem with it, but that, in fact, he rarely felt seen by Lates.

With his next observation the room went silent. He commented that in his experience, "Lates treat Earlies like pets." People from that Intensive group have told me that they learned more about Earlies with those few words than from all of my teaching.

A Middle-Axis Vignette: "God gives us two options."

Some Middles can feel inadequate when comparing themselves to the creativity of Earlies or the sophistication of Lates. I've noted how the humor of Middles often has an irreverent edge. A very Middle Middle in one of the Intensive groups—a cattle farmer—was particularly adept at humorously putting Earlies and Lates in their place.

Food in the intensives was handled potluck-style with everyone bringing something to contribute. The cattle farmer would each time bring beef in some form. Partly he did this because beef was what he most readily had to share. But there was also a more personal reason. Several of the Earles and Lates in the group were vegetarians and he wanted to be clear that he was not at all embarrassed about his means of livelihood. To emphasize his point, on the first weekend he mentioned with a grin that he always named his cattle. At each weekend gathering he would note, as an aside, just who it was we were eating that month.

A couple of moments particularly stand out in reflecting on the at once playful and serious (and very Middle) way he related to the group. One came in response to a comment someone made about his bald head. He turned to the group, smiled, and responded, "God gives us two options. We can have hair, or we can be hung like a horse." I'm sure no one in the group ever again looked at his bald pate in quite the same way.

The second moment came at the meal celebrating the last weekend of the Intensive. It was a special event and everyone brought a favorite dish. The pertinent question was obvious, now that the group was familiar with his tradition and group bonds had become close. Those who ate meat wanted to know who from his herd we were eating this month. He looked up at the group, paused, and with a sly smile responded, I named him Charley (how the group referred to me.) Everyone found it a great concluding gesture. And certainly it was a gesture that only a Middle would consider.

A Late-Axis Vignette: "Earlies think we are so superficial."

The third example again comes from the group exercise I noted with the Early-Axis example. Now the Lates were giving the presentation and the Earlies and Middles were the ones asking questions. I always encourage those doing the questioning to probe deeply and not pull punches. And in this case they did their job particularly well.

One of my faculty was facilitating the process. Being a Late, she also got to be in the group on the receiving end of the questioning.

Like most Lates, she was adept at always seeming strong and together. But I could tell that some of the questioning, particularly from a few of the Earlies, was getting to her. At one point she responded in a way that surprised me and everyone else in the room. Suddenly she stopped what she had been saying, and with tears in her eyes, exclaimed, "You Earlies think we are so superficial!"

Embarrassed at her reaction, she quickly pulled herself back together. But it opened up a great discussion. We talked about how good Lates can be at hiding their vulnerability. We also discussed the important difference between being embodied more from the surface layers of experience and what people imply with the word "superficial." My colleague found this distinction valuable for her sense of security and self worth. And the Earlies and Middles in the room found it helpful for fully appreciating what was unique and important in the Late-Axis contribution.

Comparative Vignettes

The three short descriptions that follow contrast people who have made related kinds of societal contributions, but with the gifts of different temperaments.

An Innovation Vignette: Nikola Tesla and Thomas Edison

Fig. 6-1   Nikola Tesla: by Napoleon Sarony, Wikimedia Commons; Thomas Edison: Perry-Castañeda Library, Wikimedia Commons

Before his name came to be associated with automobiles, few people had heard of Nikola Tesla. But Tesla, in fact, was one of America's most important inventors. The alternating current that propels much of our lives was a product of his fertile mind. And he anticipated much that makes today's wireless communication possible.

During their lifetimes, Tesla and Thomas Edison were often in conflict. The fact that Tesla was an Early/Upper and Edison a Middle/Upper with a touch of Late helps make sense of it. Tesla was the mad genius (sometimes to the point of outright craziness). Edison was the engineer. He is widely known today as one of history's most prolific inventors. He was also a rather ruthless businessman.

The most well-known conflict concerned the advent of electric power. Edison had invented direct current as a safer alternative to the high voltage arc lamps that were beginning to bring light to the cities. He also invented a light bulb that could make use of it. Soon the Edison Illuminating Company was providing safe light to Manhattan and beginning to spread to other cities around the country. However, direct current had a problem: It is very difficult to transmit over long distances. Alternating current provided an alternative and Tesla, with his brilliant mathematical mind, worked out the mechanics for an alternating current generating motor. It proved much the superior system. Edison was extremely competitive, had invested a great deal in direct current, and was ready to do whatever winning required. That went so far as mounting a dramatic campaign to convince people that alternating current was dangerous. But alternating current is what we most often use today.

What ultimately transpired for each man is not surprising given their different temperaments. Edison is famous today for his multitude of practical inventions such as the telephone, the phonograph, and the motion picture camera. Tesla, in combination with Westinghouse (Edison's competitor), profited well from his discovery. But he died a relatively unknown and nearly penniless man, in large part because of later grand experiments that ended in failure. We see two very different kinds of creative people, each with a particular kind of contribution.

A Leadership Vignette: Neville Chamberlain and Winston Churchill

The differing temperaments of Neville Chamberlain and Winston Churchill played a significant role in the beginnings of the Second World War and directly affected how the war played out. Both had a lot of Middle/Upper in their personalities, as most politicians do. But Chamberlain also had a lot of Later/Upper/Inner in his makeup. Churchill's temperament was very much Middle/Upper/Outer—almost to the point of caricature.

Fig. 6-2 Neville Chamberlin: National Portrait Gallery, Wikimedia; Sir Winston Churchill: Yousuf Karsh, Library and Archives Canada, Wikimedia Commons

Most people remember Neville Chamberlain's time as England's prime minister for his appeasement stance toward Nazi Germany, in particular his signing of the Munich agreement that ceded the German speaking Sudetenland region of Czechoslovakia to Hitler. Arguably it was the Late/Upper/Inner part of his temperament that made such a stance possible. There are academics who think Chamberlain has been judged harshly by history, that England was not prepared for war in those early years. But had he been a Middle/Upper/Outer like Churchill, it is most unlikely that we would have seen such a compromising response to Nazi aggression.

Winston Churchill came in as prime minister and provided just the kind of no-nonsense, inspired leadership that the English people needed to survive the very difficult early years of the war and to ultimately prevail. His temperament was a perfect match for the task, and he is appropriately venerated for his contribution. But it is unlikely that he would have been a good leader in other circumstances. With his extreme temperament, he was uncompromising in his positions and an unapologetic imperialist.

Film Directors: Wes Anderson, John Ford and Tom Ford

Fig 6-3 Wes Anderson (2018): Martin Kraft, Wikimedia Commons; John Ford (1946): Wikimedia Commons; Tom Ford (2009): Nicolas Genin, Wikimedia Commons

Three film directors provide an example from the arts. Their personality styles are reflected both in the content of their work and the characteristic ways in which they worked.

Wes Anderson is Early to the core. His films are recognized for their eccentricity and unique visual and narrative style. He is best known for his early works Bottle Rocket (1996) and Rushmore (1998), and for the The Grand Budapest Hotel (2014) for which he received an Academy Award nomination. His films often contain themes of innocence and its loss, grief and challenge, and the goings on of dysfunctional families.

Anderson's approach is eccentric not just in its content. but also with regard to the filmmaking process. In an interview about the making of The French Dispatch, which was filmed in a small town in France, he reflected: "What I like to do is go to a place and have us all live there and become a real local sort of production, like a little theater company—everything works better for me that way." He went further to observe that, "I often employ people with their own pets in the background."

John Ford was the quintessential Middle. Before becoming a film director, he was a naval officer. Besides films for which he received Academy Awards such as How Green Was My Valley and The Quiet Man, we recognize him for directing Westerns such as Stagecoach, My Darling Clementine, Rio Grande, and The Man Who Shot Liberty Valance. He often framed his shots against a harsh and vast terrain. During World War II, he made documentaries for the Navy and was present on Omaha Beach on D-Day. His career spanned more than fifty years, and included more than one-hundred-forty films. Consistent with his Middle-Axis temperament, John Ford had long-term working relationships with many of his actors, such as John Wayne, Henry Fonda, Maureen O'Hara, and James Stewart. His production crew worked with him for decades.

Tom Ford, who directed the movie A Single Man, is very much the Late/Lower/Outer. Before taking part in the movie industry, he was creative director of Gucci and Yves Saint Laurent. There, in the 1990's, he turned explicit sexuality into high fashion. In a 2009 article in The New York Times, Laura Holson wrote of his entry into the Beverly Hills Hotel to meet a friend in a way that could only describe a Late. "His stride was deliberate, arms slightly bent to frame his rigid torso. As he approached the table he removed his tea-colored sunglasses. He smelled like vanilla bean."

After the release of A Single Man, several associates of Tom Ford expressed surprise that he would make such an emotion-filled film. Ford described the response of one friend who he'd known for fifteen years who commented, "I've always thought of you as a beautiful black lacquered box with a platinum handle from the 1920s, but I never knew there was anything inside the box." Mr. Ford's response similarly expressed surprise: "You've been my friend and you did not know there was anything more than the surface?"

A Relationship Vignette: An Early, a Middle, and a Late

The three descriptions that follow were contributed by Lyn Dillman, a teacher of young children who is skilled with the personality typology. I will Include some of her more general observations about temperament and children in Chapter Eight. The words that follow are hers.

General Thoughts

As a teacher, I have found the Creative Systems Personality Typology extremely helpful in responding to the various learning needs of children. Working with people of any age, I have found it important to remind myself that we each understand our worlds from very different places. It would be easy to fall into the trap of expecting others to experience that world as I do. The Creative Systems Personality Typology has given me a framework to at least attempt to understand my students 'points of view.

Katie—A Late

Katie was one of my kindergarten students. She was one of those children who always seemed to look neat and put together (not typical for a six year old) even after playing outdoors. She was a bright child who quickly picked up new concepts and was meticulous in her work—so meticulous that a mistake in writing or drawing would sometimes lead to a near meltdown. It was very difficult for her to move forward if she was unhappy with some aspect of her project.

Coming from more Middle/Inner sensibilities, I was very forgiving of learning errors and considered them part of the process. Though I couldn't fully identify with Katie's feelings, recognizing that she was a Late allowed me to sympathize and see how important it was to her to have no mistakes in her work. In fact, it was necessary to remedy them before she could proceed. Her mother, also a Late, was the one who came up with a solution. She invented the "word band-aid" and I implemented it with Katie. A piece of white sticky-back paper did the trick. I would cut it to size and she would stick it over the mistake which she could then correct and move on. Knowing the personality typology allowed me the insight not to dismiss Katie's concern.

Billie—An Early

Another student stands out because of her Early traits. She was easy to spot as an Early because she rarely wore shoes. All year long, she was often barefoot, indoors and out. Billie came to our learning community at the age of nine from a school where there was great concern about her not reading or completing other work. She was not acting out, but she was unhappy and her parents recognized that she was not able to thrive in that particular environment. A comment that she made to me after she had spent a little time in our class group was very telling: "I don't think my last teacher really saw me."

Though she loved listening to books read aloud, Billie had challenges in learning to read and was diagnosed with dyslexia. With additional tutoring and hard work on her part she became an avid reader. Had I not understood CST personality styles, I might have worried more about Billie myself. She was reluctant to write or read during class time and often seemed to be doing very little learning. But I knew she was bright and she clearly had her own interests so I gave her lots of room to follow her own path. She felt very much a part of our learning community and was never disruptive to others. Because our community taught children kindergarten through high school, I had the privilege to see Billie grow into a dedicated student with many interests. She played cello, loved to bake, designed some of her own clothes, and excelled in her academic classes. As a senior in high school, she still often didn't wear shoes.

Matt—A Middle

Middle children stand out less in classroom settings because most schools are biased towards Middle sensibilities. Because I taught in a more open environment which did not operate with a highly structured curriculum, I did have some Middle students who struggled with this freedom. Often it manifested in difficulty getting started with specific tasks. For much of the day, it was up to the children to choose what they worked on and when. Such open-ended scheduling was difficult for some of the more Middle learners. They often benefited if they were given a starting point or had a conversation with me to decide a first step.

One student I taught exemplified a common pitfall for Middles. He was doing very little of his own work, but was very engaged in helping a friend get his work done. Matt was ten at the time so he was old enough to join a conference with me and his mother. Being a Middle myself, I identified with the tactic of distracting oneself by helping others. I shared my own experience with Matt during the conference and asked if he found it easier to work on his friend's project than his own. He sheepishly but honestly answered yes. It wasn't a cure, but the insight allowed a conversation about how he might shift to his own work.

An Organizational Vignette

In Chapter Four, I made reference to an internal think tank group that I led years back within Seattle's public television station. I include a brief description as a vignette because it reflects a way of working that can be applied in many contexts.

Our task in meeting regularly over the course of three years was to grapple with questions pertinent to the future of public media. In bringing the group together, I applied an approach that I have often used in organizational settings, one that draws on the power of temperament differences. I selected the group from throughout the station, choosing high Capacitance individuals from each department—administration, tech, production, marketing, and even a janitor.

Because I drew the group from different parts of the organization, the whole of temperament diversity was well represented. And because those who would need to explicitly make decisions were in the room, the group needed no formal authority. It became a change-making body just through the dynamism of the interactions.

The initial setup of such a group requires a basic understanding of temperament differences and the ability to effectively evaluate Capacitance. And facilitation requires enough culturally mature capacity that one can effectively provide guidance in a group with such broad diversity. But once those criteria are met, the approach proves powerful and relatively straightforward. Just by virtue of the group's makeup, the kinds of questions addressed, and the nature of the facilitation, the approach directly supports a culturally mature contribution.

A Personal Scale Developmental Vignette: Parents as a "Tag Team"

I've noted that Creative Systems Theory is unique as a framework in including both developmental (Patterning in Time) and here-and-now (Patterning in Space) concepts. The next vignette illustrates how an appreciation for both Patterning in Time and Patterning in Space distinctions can provide important insight. It again comes from my personal experience, in this case my relationship with my parents while growing up.

My mother was an Early (primarily a visual artist). In contrast, as I've noted, my father was dead-on Middle. When I was a young child (in my Early-Axis stage developmentally), my mother was an exceptional parent. She was particularly adept at engaging my Early sensibilities. Together, we immersed ourselves in the imaginal. We would make and act puppets, create songs, take long walks in nature. While I appreciated my father during this time, the connection was not nearly as strong. I felt the solidity of his presence. And I knew he cared. But we just didn't seem to have that much in common.

An odd thing happened as I reached age seven or eight. My mother turned back to her artist studio. It was almost as if she was saying, "OK, I've done what I know how to do." And suddenly I felt less interest and significance in what we had done together. What had been a rich connection almost disappeared.

I might have felt loss and loneliness if it weren't for my dad. Just in time, there he was with fishing pole and hiking boots ready to accompany me on a whole different kind of creative adventure. Developmentally, I was preparing to move into Middle-Axis, and I had a good Middle right there and ready to support and teach in just the ways I was needing. Prior to this, I had never really seen him, and he had had no real way to connect with me. In part this was because I had been at an Early-Axis stage in development. But, as much, it was a function of the fact that temperament-wise I have much more Early in me than Middle. Only with my beginning engagement with more Middle-Axis developmental tasks was there enough shared Middleness for us to connect.

Because of their contrasting personality styles, my parents made a great developmental tag team. Now that I have Creative Systems Theory temperament concepts to draw on, it is fun to look back. I am able to more deeply appreciate each of my parents—both their particular gifts and each of their limitations and absurdities.

A More Cultural Scale Developmental Vignette: Mikhail Gorbachev and Vladimir Putin

Contrasting the leadership of Mikhail Gorbachev and Vladimir Putin helps bring together multiple kinds of distinctions that I've proposed are important in applying the typology. If we are to fully make sense of their places in history and effectively reflect on implications for the future, we need to include Patterning in Time in the sense of cultural development, Capacitance, and also temperament.

Fig 6-4   Mikhail Gorbachev in the White House Library: White House Photographic Collection, Wikimedia Commons; Vladimir Putin (2022): Wikimedia Commons

Contrasting the leadership of Mikhail Gorbachev and Vladimir Putin helps bring together multiple kinds of distinctions that I've proposed are important in applying the typology. If we are to fully make sense of their places in history and effectively reflect on implications for the future, we need to include

Patterning in Time in the sense of cultural development, Capacitance, and also temperament.

In other writings, I've compared the roles of Gorbachev and Putin as a way to illustrate the importance of Patterning in Time considerations. I've proposed that Gorbachev, while an insightful thinker, was ahead of his time in relation to the Soviet people. One consequence is that, today, he is not widely respected in his homeland. And he was arguably not a successful leader. It was not his intent to have his actions result in the breakup of the old Soviet Union.

I've also suggested that Putin, in a Patterning Time sense, was a better fit for what the Russian people then needed. I think of Russia as residing in the Middle-Axis substage of Late-Axis Culture. During this period in culture, the most effective governmental form tends to be the benevolent dictatorship. Putin sat more comfortably in that developmental reality. And, at least initially, his dictatorial actions were largely benevolent. Today his inability to manifest needed Capacitance has resulted in behavior that is decidedly regressive. But at the time, he was the better match.

While Patterning in Time observations capture much of the difference, I think Patterning in Space personality style observations are ultimately just as pertinent. It was not just that Gorbachev was further along developmentally; he also had a significant amount of Late-Axis along with Middle-Axis in his personality makeup. I've emphasized that no personality style has an advantage when it comes to development. But I suspect that the Late-Axis element in Gorbachev's temperament made it easier for him to understand the West and also to see how democratic principles might have a place in his people's future. Putin's temperament, in contrast, is almost entirely Middle-Axis. The result is a person who is much more nationalist by inclination and more naturally comfortable with an authoritarian approach.

In our time, this combination of developmental and temperament characteristics along with Putin's limited Capacitance makes for an extremely dangerous mix. Putin is highly vulnerable to interpreting history in terms of violation by the West and to seeing the future only as nationalistic struggle. It is not surprising that we might see the kind of inhumane military exploits that we witness today in Ukraine. And with Russia's great stockpiles of nuclear arms, we confront the possibility of global catastrophe. I agree with the best of Russia experts that getting beyond today's dangers will likely only be possible with Putin somehow being replaced. Drawing on Patterning in Time, Patterning in Space, and Capacitance variables can help us think about the kind of person who might best replace him. It can also help us think about how best to engage that leader if cooperation and peace are to be possible.

CHAPTER SEVEN

Exercises and Comparisons

Two ways of introducing the typology can prove particularly helpful. Hands-on, experiential teaching methods provide one of the best ways to communicate the typology's basic structure. And comparative observations that highlight distinctions can help solidify initial learnings.

Experiential Approaches

Because Creative Systems ideas conceive in terms of the whole of who we are—not only our behaviors and beliefs—psychological tests as we traditionally think of them are not that useful with the typology. In the end, the most effective tool for making distinctions is another human being. Partly because of this, and partly just because of the added depth of understanding that comes from engaging understanding more experientially, I've tended through the years to teach about the typology through more hands-on approaches. Here are a few that I've found particularly useful when working with groups.

Brainstorming Questions

I often get started by presenting simple brainstorming questions to the group that help highlight the simple fact of how different we can be from one another. I encourage people to reflect and then to write down their responses. Then I have them break up into groups of three or four and share responses. Later, I bring the large group back together and invite people to share examples of responses that surprised them and that highlighted differences.

Here is a sampling of possible questions: What might people say most stands out with your personality? What things in life are most important to you? What are your most common fears? When you feel envy, what is it most commonly about? What kind of clothes feel most like you? What sports do you most enjoy watching or taking part in? What is something that would make you feel seen and understood if you received it as a gift? What kind of pets have you had in your life? What are your preferences when it comes to music, art, and entertainment. What is one thing about you that a person might call an idiosyncrasy? What do you do to relax? What qualities do you most value in other people? What do you like to read and why? If you were going to insult someone, how would you do it? What kinds of people do you have the hardest time with? What turns you on romantically/sexually?

Personality Style Cards and the Diversity Game

I often use a set of Personality Style Cards, developed at the Institute to introduce the typology. One side of each card has an image, quote, saying, or observation. The other side has a diagram that identifies the personality styles that would be most likely to respond positively to it.

Application of the cards is limited only by the imagination of the user. At the simplest level, a person can start by picking eight or ten cards that "ring true," along with four or five cards where this is definitely not the case. The person can then look on the reverse of the cards to see the personality styles that the content on the cards most often reflect.

When working with a group, I may use five or six decks of cards so that there are enough to go around. After choosing cards, I have people read both their "rings true" and "not me" cards aloud. I invite people to talk about why, in each instance, they chose the cards they did. And I encourage others in the larger group to ask curiosity questions.

I've included a few examples of cards below. The full set of cards is available to download on the CSPT website (www.CSPThome.org). Feel free to make your own set.

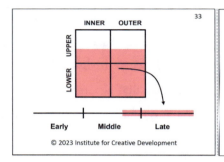

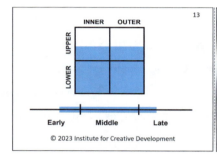

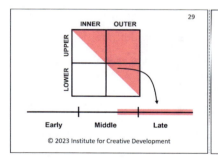

THE CREATIVE SYSTEMS PERSONALITY TYPOLOGY

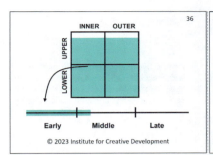

I love things primal: the roar of the ocean, the musky smell that lingers after sex.

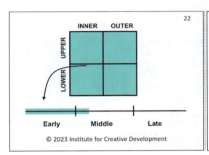

"If you have any notion of where you are going, you will never get there."
— Joan Miro

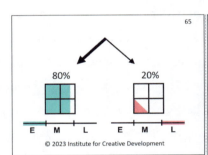

I really value solitude. It nourishes me and brings me close to the spiritual and the creative in things. It's funny, I often feel least alone when I'm by myself.

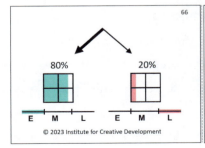

"Make your ego porous. Will is of little importance, complaining is nothing, fame is nothing. Openness, patience, receptivity, solitude is everything."
—Rainer Marie Rilke

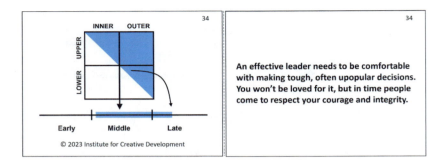

An effective leader needs to be comfortable with making tough, often unpopular decisions. You won't be loved for it, but in time people come to respect your courage and integrity.

Name That Tune

I call a group approach I've often used at the Institute "Name That Tune." To start, a person from the group selects someone that they know well personally, but that others in the group have not met. They are then instructed to go out of the room, take a moment to connect with their experience of the person they have selected, and to return as that person—taking on his or her voice quality, gestures, and values.

The group then interviews the mystery person. Their job is to guess the person's temperament with the smallest number of questions. The approach is a great way to deepen understanding of the temperament framework. It can also be great fun. "Name That Tune" requires at least some beginning familiarity with the typology. And it is best when facilitated by someone who has experience with the typology. But this book provides enough background that people should be able to try it out.

Cross-Temperament Conversations

I made reference to one of the most informative—and often provocative—group approaches with a couple of the previous chapter's vignettes. It engages the different axes directly in conversation with one another.

The exercise starts with the facilitator breaking the large group into three subgroups by Axis. The subgroups then go off to separate rooms with a list of questions to answer. Questions span across realms of experience and range from the casual to the probing: What do you most like to do for fun? What beliefs are most important to you? If someone wanted to irritate you, how might they best go about it? Who are some of the people that you most admire, and why? What are others most likely to misunderstand about you? How do you know if someone loves you?

After taking time to write answers to the questions, people within the three axis groups share their responses with one another, noting particularly interesting commonalities and differences. The facilitator encourages the small groups to let conversations proceed in whatever directions seem of interest. This can take several hours.

Eventually, the facilitator brings the three groups back together. Each temperament group, in turn, takes their place on a "stage" set up at one end of the room. Each group first does a presentation to help the other temperament groups better understand their particular personality style's reality. They then entertain curiosity questions from the other two groups.

There are always surprises, and often dramatic ones. Even though participants are familiar with the typology, they can find it startling how different the answers to simple questions can be. I particularly enjoy hearing people's responses to the "how do you know if people love you" question. They can be so varied—even totally at odds—that it can be hard to imagine how people with different temperaments could ever have successful relationships.

These group interactions must be facilitated carefully. We don't realize how much of the violation people experience in life has its roots in personality style differences. Remember how potentially charged some exchanges became in the previous vignettes—with words like "Lates treat Earlies like pets" and "You Earlies think we Lates are so superficial." It is important to maintain an atmosphere of inquiry and mutual respect.

Comparisons

A good way to become facile with the typology is to compare and contrast. Here I will first offer a few "diagnostic terms," words that we tend to associate with one particular temperament axis. I will then make some comparative observations that have to do with motivations, beliefs, and aesthetic preferences. And finally I will turn to an odd assortment of fun comparisons—from cars, to shoe preferences, to bumper stickers.

Diagnostic Terms

We commonly associate certain words and phrases with particular personality styles. Some are so particular that we can think of them as diagnostic. If we encounter them in a novel or a news report, the temperament of the person being referred to is obvious. Others are more generally descriptive. These could

Early Terms

Diagnostic words and phrases: Quirky, earthy, free spirit, magical, visionary, wild, creature-like, mysterious, eccentric, whimsical, gangly, willowy, spontaneous, brooding, untamed, charismatic, having a touch of madness, marches to the beat of one's own drum.

Other common descriptive words and phrases: Inspired, peculiar, absent-minded, sensitive, immodest, indelicate, hedonistic, independent, intuitive, colorful, pagan, unconstrained, original, pensive, portly, diffident, shy, lone wolf, curious, sensitive, insightful, meditative, open, childlike, tactile, contemplative.

Middle Terms

Diagnostic words and phrases: Steadfast, down to earth, devoted, brash, plucky, gruff, loyal, demanding, thrifty, plainspoken, hard-headed, prudent, strapping, no nonsense, autocratic, hardy, wiry, vigorous, salt of the earth.

Other common descriptive words and phrases: Dependable, compassionate, protective, responsible, thorough, sensible, committed, adventurous, determined, organized, firm, traditional, strategic, reliable, patient, loyal, practical, cooperative, faithful, demanding, supportive, action-oriented, fair, principled, persistent, constant, humble, capable, unselfish, undaunted, tolerant, thrifty, contrary, oppositional, stable, trustworthy, tenacious, strong-willed, stalwart, sturdy, buxom.

Late Terms:

Diagnostic words and phrases: Refined, sophisticated, scholarly, classy, dapper, intellectual, vivacious, fact-oriented, theatrical, stylish, elevated, impeccable, lavish, diplomatic, professorial, glamorous, classy, elegant, cultivated, suave, chic, savvy.

Other common descriptive words and phrases: Enterprising, detail-oriented, status-seeking, opulent, precise, outgoing, perfectionistic, excitable, discerning, sharp, impeccable, flighty, coy, flamboyant, effusive, competitive, romantic, haughty, ambitious, fashionable, extravagant, sociable, clever, detached, analytical, trendy, meticulous, gregarious, logical, quick, sharp, sexy, highbrow, dramatic, classic, stately, fabulous, genteel.

What Motivates Them

Some of the most defining differences concern what, for different temperaments most motivates actions and underlies values. Again, there can be great diversity, but we can also make some general observations:

Earlies tend to be most motivated by circumstances that provide a sense of inspiration and calling. They are drawn to activities that reflect possibility, involve innovation, and offer a feeling of connectedness with larger purpose. Often we see a valuing of relatedness with nature and the untamed.

Middles tend to value activities that make a concrete contribution, most often of an interpersonal sort. More than other temperaments, Middles can also find hard work in itself motivating. Middles can be particularly attracted to activities that provide a sense of control or power. In a way not found with other temperaments, they can also find satisfaction in constancy and support of the status quo.

Lates tend to value individual accomplishment and intellectual or material achievement. Being articulate can be an important mark of significance. And competition in their field can be a strong motivator. More than other temperaments, Lates tend to be aware of appearances and can be driven by the importance of looking good in the eyes of others. Of all temperaments, they are the most likely to value status and celebrity.

 be applied to other temperaments, but if you wanted to write about someone, they would be on your list of possible descriptive terms.

Beliefs

I promised in the previous chapter to link other kinds of Patterning in Space observations to personality style distinctions. Here I do so briefly for political and religious beliefs.

Political Advocacy and Belief

With political beliefs, we can make a very rough Patterning in Space association between more archetypally feminine sensibilities and liberal advocacy and between more archetypally masculine sensibilities and advocacy of a more conservative sort. MSNBC commentator Chris Matthews once referred to the Democratic party in the U.S. as the "mommy party" and the Republican party as the "daddy party."

Temperament helps us fill out this most basic observation. If Earlies choose to engage the political world (often politics feels too Middle/Upper or

Late/Upper for Earlies to get actively involved), they tend to be liberal or progressive/populist in their beliefs. They also tend to be more drawn to issues than partisan advocacy—and here to particular kinds of issues (for example, peace, the environment, or social justice).

It is Middles who are likely to feel most at home with the struggles of conventional partisanship. Middle/Upper/Outers tend toward the conservative—that strong identification with control. Middle/Upper/Inners, with their additional touch of the archetypally feminine, can be either liberal or conservative. Middle/Lower/Outers are often the most ardently conservative, with beliefs of an extreme right-wing sort being common. While Middle/Lower/Inners can also be conservative (traditional values remain strong), they may also identify with liberal values such workers's rights or identification with the underprivileged.

Late/Uppers, particularly if they have a fair dose of Middle/Upper, can also be quite effective in the political sphere. Late/Upper/Outers tend to be conservative out of identification with social and economic advantage. In contrast, Late/Upper/Inners and Late/Lowers tend to be liberal. With Late/Upper/Inners this reflects their tendency toward humanistic values. With Late/Lowers, it more reflects their identification with the feeling side of experience.

Spiritual/Religious Belief

We can map a similar set of Patterning in Space relationships with regard to religion. Creative Systems Theory makes the basic Pattern in Space observation that spiritual/religious belief reflects connection with the archetypally feminine as it manifests within culture as a system. (Such belief is about oneness as opposed to difference, and, in particular, how we experience it collectively.[1])

Again, we can fill out this basic observation by adding the variable of temperament.

Earlies often describe themselves as spiritual rather than religious. And their beliefs can be untraditional. Earlies may find particular meaning in meditation or with simply being in nature. Earlies are also the most likely to feel affinity with Eastern forms of thought and practice. People who identify with Wiccan beliefs will most often have Early/Lower personalities.

Middles are the most apt to identify with religion in a traditional institutional sense. The more conservative religious traditions often hold particular appeal—fundamentalist Protestant, more orthodox Judaism, the more traditional of Catholic or Islamic views; but the greater portion of attendees in all but the most liberal of congregations tend to be Middles. The beliefs of Christian religious cults tend to have their roots in the early parts of Middle-Axis.

Lates tend to be more secular in their sensibilities, but they also can be church or synagogue goers. When they do attend services, they will often opt for a religious affiliation that is more philosophical than ritualistic or moralistic. They may also chose a faith tradition or congregation that could be associated with higher status.

Aesthetic Preferences

One of the best ways to engage the less conscious aspects of temperament differences is to look at aesthetic preferences, as with music or humor.

---

[1] My book Creative Systems Theory includes a detailed look at how the theory explains the role of religious belief in the human story.

Musical Preferences

Early preferences: Jazz, rock and roll, folk and world music, some classical if the personality is Upper Pole, and most more alternative forms. (Miles Davis, Bob Dylan, Woody Guthrie, B.B. King, Joni Mitchell, Bob Marley, Kurt Cobain, Billie Eilish. or Janis Joplin.)

Middle preferences: Country western, rock, punk rock, rap, marches, and for some Uppers, opera and classical. (Johnny Cash, Dolly Parton, John Philip Souza, Johnny Rotten, Ice Cube—and perhaps Luciano Pavarotti.)

Late preferences: Classical, pop, jazz, some rock, Broadway musicals, and easy listening (Leonard Bernstein and the NewYork Philharmonic, Yo-Yo Ma, Frank Sinatra, the Beatles, Rogers and Hammerstein, Tony Bennet, and Billie Holiday).

Preferences in Humor

The kind of humor a person prefers similarly provides a quite reliable, less conscious kind of indicator. Below, I've listed a few well known humorists by personality style. People with related personality styles are particularly likely to find them funny:

Early humorists: Charlie Chaplin, Jonathan Winters, George Carlin, Lily Tomlin, Bill Murray, David Letterman.

Middle humorists: Will Rogers, Jay Leno, Jimmy Kimmel, Carol Burnette, Rodney Dangerfield, Amy Schumer, Richard Prior.

Late humorists: Johnny Carson, John Stewart, Lucille Ball, Tina Fey, Steve Carell, Dean Martin, and Bob Hope.

Sports and Recreational Activities

People of particular temperaments are especially likely to enjoy and participate in certain sports and recreational activities:

For Earlies: Running, skateboarding, rock climbing, volleyball, frisbee, hiking, snow-boarding, swimming, hang gliding, rowing, hacky sack, bicycling (and, particularly diagnostic, riding a unicycle).

For Middles: Football, fishing, hunting, baseball, ice hockey, rugby, bowling, soccer, roller derby, basketball, rodeo sports, golf, track and field, horseback riding, gymnastics, NASCAR-style auto racing, boating.

For Lates: Tennis, golf, ice skating, synchronized swimming, skiing, polo, lacrosse, ballroom dancing, billiards, more formal equestrian sports such as dressage, horse racing (as owners), Formula One-style auto racing, yachting.

Preferred Mind-Altering Activities

People with different temperaments can feel particular attraction to certain substances (and also practices) that alter mental or emotional states. The activities mirror in their effects the experiences that each temperament most associates with meaning. Below I've listed chemical substances that certain individuals can find especially attractive—and sometimes addictive.[2] And in parentheses, I've added consciousness-altering practices that for each axis can create a related kind of felt experience.

For Earlies: Cannabis and other psychedelics, alcohol (along with yoga, meditation, and being in nature).

For Middles: Beer, whiskey, uppers and downers (along with prayer, watching sports, and craftwork).

For Lates: Fine wine, cocktails, Scotch, cocaine (along with traveling, theater, and the symphony).

---

2 In Chapter Nine, I will look more specifically at addiction.

Some Particularly Odd and Fun Comparisons

Looking at how differences can be reflected in odd everyday choices adds some fun, further perspective. As alway, we must be careful in the enjoyment of caricature not to be simplistic. As Einstein cautioned, "It is important to make things as simple as possible, but no simpler."

Pets

Earlies: Of all temperaments, Earlies tend to be most naturally fond of animals. Often they have many pets when they are children, and they frequently make unusual pet choices. Owning an iguana is pretty diagnostic. My favorite pet as a child was a duck.

Middles: Of all temperaments, Middles tend to be most naturally attracted to dogs and often own large ones. Working dogs can have a special appeal (perhaps a Labrador Retriever). Middle/Inners are often particularly fond of cats. And people who own horses are most often Middles (unless they race them).

Lates: Lates tend to have less of a natural affinity for animals. But Late/Lowers in particular can be especially fond of cats. Late/Lowers are also some of the people most likely to own dogs of the miniature variety. There are also certain larger, generally purebred dogs that Lates in particular may appreciate (a standard poodle, for example).

Cars

Earlies: Earlies would often rather ride a bike or take the transit than drive a car. But certain cars, like older Volkswagens and Subarus, can have special attraction for Earlies. And every now and then, you will find Earlies who have a fondness for sports cars, particularly classic ones. Earlies are the most likely to name their cars.

Middles: Middles tend to like cars that are reliable and basic—a Toyota, a Ford or Chevy. Most minivans are owned by Middles. In certain parts of the the U.S., the fact that a car is American-made can add to its appeal. SUV's are increasingly popular with Middles. And for many Middles, their car is a truck. "Car guys" tend to be Middles.

Lates: Lates tend to be attracted to more upscale brands—BMW, Lexus, Audi, Mercedes, Porsche. Teslas and other higher end electric cars can also have appeal (as they do for some more well off Earlies). Lates are the most likely to buy new cars and tend to keep their cars clean and well maintained.

Clothing Preferences

Clothing preferences can be quite specific to temperament. Here I will limit observations to shoes as they can be particularly diagnostic. (You might try adding a related list for other kinds of attire.)

Early: Comfort is the highest priority for Earlies when it comes to footwear. They may wear sandals or sneakers. Earlies who spend a lot of time in the out-of-doors often wear hiking boots (and choose them carefully). Earlies are the most likely to enjoy going barefoot.

Middle: Middles tend to prefer practical shoes. For the workplace, that could be loafers or low heels. For everyday, that might be tennis shoes. Middles who can afford them can be attracted to "Air Jordans," and the like.

Late: Lates are the most likely to wear more formal shoes, such as wingtips for men and high heels for women. Lates are also most likely to have special shoes for particular occasions, such as deck shoes for boating (and also to have extensive shoe collections—remember Imelda Marcos).

And Bumper Stickers

Early: While bumper stickers are more common on Middle-Axis vehicles, when an Early gets into them, they flourish with a characteristic boundaryless flair. My favorite: "Visualize Whirled Peas."

Middle: Bumper stickers are almost diagnostically Middle/Lower: Here one finds the most and the best. Some of my favorites: "I brake for beer"; "Children: Tired of being harassed by your stupid parents? Act now! Move out. Get a job. Pay your own bills while you still know everything"; and "Legalize Lutefisk."

Lates: Late-Axis people are very unlikely to have bumper stickers on their cars. You will on occasion find vanity plates.

CHAPTER EIGHT

Application With Children

I've noted how the typology is directly applicable to understanding temperament differences in children. In fact, it is often with children that personality style differences are most clear. And certainly it is often in work with children that an appreciation of such differences can be most consequential. Below, I've included pieces written by a couple of skilled teachers who have applied the CSPT in their teaching efforts.

Lyn Dillman has worked with me through the years in developing the typology. Here she introduces how she thinks about temperament with young children and describes teaching approaches that she has found work the best with children of various personality styles. She ends with a summary of the strengths that she has observed with each temperament and the particular learning challenges that each faces.

Teresa Piddington has worked with Lyn in teaching the typology and its application for use in school settings. Here she describes how she engages children of various personality styles differently in teaching writing to second graders.

For this book's task, reflections from work with children have an added benefit. Because personality characteristics tend to present themselves with particular purity when we are young, observations with children help us get at the heart of what is important for each temperament and provide a useful kind of summary.

Lyn Dillman: Temperament and Learning

When I was in graduate school, I wrote a paper on the premise that children's temperaments should predict something about their learning styles. At the time I recall that my instructor thought I had not taken the idea far enough. In retrospect, I had in fact barely scratched the surface of what seems obvious to me now.

As I sat down to approach this question once again using the personality typology laid out in Creative Systems Theory, my thought was to compare and somehow link current learning style theory with this temperament typology. It then occurred to me that the link is present within the theory. The important thing is not so much finding how learning styles match up with the different temperament types as it is creating learning environments that are "friendly" and stimulating to all types of learners (i.e. personalities).

So what are those differences and what are their implications for a responsive classroom? Here I will start with brief descriptions of each temperament style as I think of it in the context of the classroom. I will follow with some thoughts about what will best serve each in a learning setting.

With Early-Axis children, the primary intelligence is imaginal intelligence, the stuff that dreams are made of. Often those we think of as "artist types" are Earlies. In the classroom, the everyday tedium of clean-up and worry about how neat a paper looks may not be on their radars, and at times they can seem a bit oblivious to others around them. But Earlies are present in their own way. Speaking of radar (no doubt an Early invented it), in this axis, along with future poets, musicians and visual artists, you will also find young computer "geeks" and math whizzes (the ones who understand far beyond most of their teachers). Earlies are very connected in their bodies and are characterized by fluid though not always graceful movement; they can appear gangly at times and almost "un-jointed."

In reading this, you might think: "That sounds like most kids I know, especially young-ones." In fact, there is a way that is true. Young children are in an Early-Axis stage of development which overlays their native temperament. But as you read the rest of the descriptions, I think you will be able to distinguish personality from developmental characteristics.

The primary intelligence of Middle-Axis is emotional intelligence. These are the children who don't need to learn empathy; they could even teach it, and from a very early age. These children are relationally oriented and often want to please the teacher. Or they may prefer to struggle with the teacher. They are generally very loyal, sometimes to a fault. This Axis is characterized by isometric tension between opposite poles. A sense of struggle and control come out of this, and oddly enough also a kind of solidness. It is as if the Middle-Axis personality is holding two walls apart. They can't move very far and probably won't move very fast, but they will be solid.

These are the children in your class who are dependable (sometimes dependably rebellious) but they tend to have a kind of stability about them. They are usually incremental learners and can sometimes appear plodding, even a bit oafish. They may contribute by modifying an existing idea or building on that of another classmate. Middles with certain aspects can be quite athletic and strong; their agility looks muscular in comparison to the more fluid agility that may be present in Early. These will be children with a strong sense of right and wrong; fairness will be important to them. They are also likely to be the ones who remember the routine of the classroom and may not like it to change. Middles typically are not the children who push themselves hard and may need external structure and spark to get them going and to help them finish things. These are often the children who say things like: "Have I done enough?"; "Can I do this tomorrow?"; "Do I have to?". Middle-Axis children generally are quite comfortable in groups and tend to do well with the group nature of a classroom. I have found that building a personal relationship with such children can go a long way in motivating them to learn.

For the Late-Axis personality, rational intelligence is primary. Lates are generally very verbally articulate and "think well on their feet." These are often children who are naturally popular in a group. Lates are graceful and often possess a natural poise and sophistication. A Late may display talent in the visual arts, music or dance. Both visual art and physical art will tend to reflect a refinement or new twist on an existing form. This differs from the Early, where you will see more raw innovation. Late-Axis children are often perfectionistic and pay keen attention to how others see them and their work. They are most alert to what is outside them; they measure things by objective criteria and are the axis most connected to form. They like things well defined, not amorphous or mushy. The part of the creative process that is home to them is the refinement of form, so the final phase of an idea or project is where they will shine.

So what does an Early need, to best enhance learning? Since Earlies tend to be self-starters and know innately what interests them, they thrive in an environment where the educator acts as a resource person. The adult in this case would provide the equipment, materials and references (from books to Internet) so that the learner can follow his or her interests. For many Early students, a helpful contribution from an adult will be guidance to follow through to the completion of a phase of learning. Since the beginning stages of creative process are the juiciest for an Early, one may find this student lingering in the beginning stages of one or many learning endeavors. A gift to an Early student may be imparting the skills to move through the Middle and Late stages of a creative project or learning task.

The innovative nature of Earlies and their ability to see vast connections among things will often result in a unique interpretation of an assignment. Because of this, teachers should be prepared to flex the boundaries and the viewpoint from which an assignment is regarded. Though this may require a stretch for teachers of a different temperament, it is necessary in order for the Early student to do his best learning and often results in fantastic and unexpected educational outcomes. This is the crux of letting an Early shine.

In addition to or perhaps as an adjunct to the support for completing a process, the Early may at times need help staying focused on a topic or area of learning. That same ability to see all things as connected may make it difficult for the Early student to choose a path and stay with it. This may require a balancing act between allowing the student to follow his or her interest and delineating a boundary to help them complete something required. When Earlies do connect with something that grabs their attention, you may find them "hyper-focused" to the exclusion of all else. Earlies do not like having their rhythms interrupted and often benefit from warning of a coming transition. Whenever possible, these students will do best if allowed to shape their own schedule regarding what to complete when. This does not mean they cannot adapt to a classroom schedule, but built into that schedule should be room for this student to self direct. Related to the flexibility I spoke of before, the culminating form of a learning assignment should be open to interpretation—perhaps a painting, a poem, an improvisational music or dance piece; the form needs to fit the "language" of the temperament.

And what does a Middle student need? Much more structure than the Earlies. Middles tend to think quite concretely and learn in the same manner. They may need help getting started, as they are most adept at the middle stages of the process. "Tell me what to do and I'll do it" might be the Middle motto. This is not to say that a Middle student will always be on task or complete their work, but they seem to benefit from clear parameters and a sense of what is expected. Unlike the Early who relishes a blank slate, the Middle student is more likely to be stymied by it.

Middles generally have a fairly easy time adapting to the typical classroom setting (this may be partly due to the fact that many of that temperament are drawn to teaching, so many classrooms reflect a Middle-Axis sensibility). Middle-Axis children do not mind rules. In fact they tend to feel safer with them and may test boundaries mercilessly if they are not clearly communicated. Middles often like learning that is active and hands-on. They seem to benefit from having a task modeled for them, but beware: They may take everything you say literally, so the trick is modeling and communicating how they should use their own thinking.

I recently asked a group of five year olds to think of their favorite number from one to nine. After going around and letting several of them share their number, I demonstrated the task we were to do with that number. I carefully selected the number four since no one had chosen it. As I went around to check their progress several of the Middle students had carefully completed the task with the number four, disregarding their favorite number. Perhaps I can chalk this up to the difficulty of communicating to five-year-olds, but it nonetheless illustrates my point.

Middles often do well in team learning situations. Ideally the team would include all of the temperaments—the Early energy to inspire, a Middle to move things along, and the Late energy to help carry them through to the finish. The completion of a process may be somewhat of a problem for Middles and is most likely to appear in the form of skimping on the final polish. As a teacher you are likely to get "B" work, where the Middle has moved through the main work phase and said "good enough." While the notion of "good enough" may be growth enhancing and healthy for a perfectionist, in a Middle it is sometimes settling for less than they are capable of doing. Middles benefit from high expectations and may need to be asked to do something again or to refine what has been done (edit that draft one more time or take time to practice that poem you are to recite).

Some Middles are encouraged by healthy competition, but fostering too much of this may cause them to back off and give up. If a Middle is more Lower and Inner, they may shut down in the face of competition even though they are very capable. Many middles will struggle with—for lack of a better word—laziness. (They also detest the word in my experience.) I think this comes from being in the middle—it is difficult to get started and energy wanes towards the finish. There is a sort of heaviness to Middle energy that provides their stability and at times their inertness. I can speak of this from my own experience as one of this temperament. Often I am inspired by ideas, but getting started to manifest them feels like an uphill climb. Then once I have started I can chug along (good Middle term) quite well until I near completion. I can then begin to feel my energy fading away from a project. Finishing can be as difficult at times as starting.

What often helps Middle-Axis students is a connection to the teacher, feeling seen and cared about. The emotional component of Middle needs to be fed in the learning environment. Building a relationship with a Middle student often provides the purpose they need to move through the creative cycle. If the sense of connection to the teacher is strong, then the Middle student will do his or her best in order not to disappoint. This "pleasing" behavior sometimes gets a bad rap in our society and in the culture of education; it can be seen as failing to foster the student's independence or uniqueness. But the gift of Middle is not uniqueness; it is emotional attentiveness, community, and stability. The desire to please others is sometimes a gift and more importantly can help connect the student to his or her own creative abilities.

What do Late-Axis children need in the classroom environment? Late-Axis children connect most readily to the end product of creation. Because of this, they are sometimes frustrated by the long road to get there. In the learning process, this can sometimes stop them before they begin, possibly rooted in their tendency for perfection; they do not wish to start something that they cannot complete beautifully. This seems especially true in the younger years when children's ability to manifest form does not match their ability to imagine it. In their mind's eye they can see the finished product, but they do not yet possess the skills to produce it. These children can often be quite protective of themselves around their perceived lack of skill and may avoid things in which they feel they cannot excel.

The Late children whom I have worked with in the five to six age range seem to benefit from having time to watch for a while. I notice that many of them like to learn new things "in private." If they feel lacking, they tend to withdraw from participation rather than be seen as incompetent. But they will go home and practice something or find ways to quietly and privately acquire a new skill. Frequently, Late children learn things quickly and are highly competent in a classroom setting. In older children you will often see a facility with words that make them good writers and orators. Late-Axis children are highly aware of who has what skills and knowledge and are often driven by a sense of competition. This can be a strong internal motivator for many Lates.

Late-Axis children seem to thrive on a certain amount of order in the classroom, both physical and relational. These children are the ones who are likely to go home and report that another child was wasting the group's time and that their opportunity for learning was being disrupted (probably not in those exact words). Late students have high expectations of their teachers and resent a teacher who is unprepared or does not stimulate their learning. Older Late-Axis students that I have talked with will say that they need to respect their teacher in order to learn from them. The basis of this respect is usually related to knowledge of the subject and organization of information being offered. As a Middle-Axis teacher of young children, I think I have made the mistake of not offering enough academic rigor for Late-Axis children. My more Middle perspective was that young children mainly need nurturance and support; but this is not true for all. In fact, though they often shy away from things they do not know, Late-Axis children seem to thrive on academic mastery. I have found that Late-Axis children benefit from opportunities to demonstrate their learning through performance. This may take the form of reading to a group what they have written, acting something out, or being videotaped.

Following is a summary of the characteristics of Early-, Middle-, and Late-Axis children as they pertain to learning with specific attention given to both strengths and challenges:

Early Axis Children

Strengths/Attributes

Innovative, imaginative, visionary, improvisational; tend to have a "whole cloth view."

Operate primarily from imaginal intelligence, but may also be quite kinesthetic (This is not the only axis where you will find this.)

Tend to be more self-focused than other-focused. If absorbed in something, they may be oblivious to others. Often these children can seem to be "in their own world."

May seek solitude more often than other children; usually feel quite comfortable alone.

Creation is original. These children are usually excited by a "blank slate."

May identify or connect with animals or nature more than humans; they are able to see the interconnectedness of things.

May be highly sensitive to sensory stimulus, e.g. loud noises, bright lights, itchy clothing (this can also show up in other axes with certain aspects present).

Generally have a low tolerance for boredom and repetitive tasks. These children seek new experience and may respond to an assignment with a completely new idea (usually a related but novel approach).

Fluidity characterizes this style; may be noted in movement, voice, and choice of clothing.

Likely to withdraw from, ignore or not register conflict unless it feels relevant to them. (They may fight vehemently for a cause they believe in.) Resolution of conflict may be nonverbal—engage in play and "watch the conflict melt away."

Marching to the beat of one's own drum typifies this axis.

Challenges

Can have difficulty relating socially. This can sometimes impede others' understanding of these children.

May have difficulty grasping social convention. These children may be surprised and hurt by a social or relational expectation that did not register for them.

May have difficulty adapting to a classroom setting that asks them to sit for long periods of time. Being able to move their bodies and sit or stand in different positions may greatly enhance their learning process.

May have difficulty with prescribed assignments, particularly if they have become repetitive. Having the flexibility to craft their own form may help.

Others may inappropriately project loneliness on these children because of their comfort with solitude and their lack of social awareness, although they may actually feel lonely at times in an environment that doesn't honor their needs.

May feel vulnerable around their creations because of a lack of boundary between themselves and what they create.

Too much external control or inflexibility may squelch the germinal creative spark.

Sometimes these children can get lost in their imagination and may need help following through to the final stages of a task. They may also need help understanding why this is important.

May have difficulty learning from a teacher whom they feel does not respect them.

Middle Axis Children

Strengths/Attributes

Solid, dependable, steady, persevering.

Relationship/other oriented; tend to be concerned about friendship and others liking them. (This does not mean that all Middle-Axis children are extroverts.) Inclusive of others. Often kind and generous, they consider others 'feelings important.

Frequently use feeling or relational language.

May be most comfortable with a prescribed structure to operate within (e.g., clear parameters for an assignment vs. open-ended). Tend to be concrete thinkers and communicators.

Creativity tends to manifest through application and modification more than origination.

May enjoy games or sports as a participant or a spectator. There is enjoyment in competition and teamwork; winning is important but not essential.

Tend to be more conforming, not wanting to stand out too much in dress or behavior. These children are not likely to be trendsetters, though they may have some awareness of what is fashionable.

May be either very adaptive or rebellious. In each case they are reacting in relation to the other person, striving to please or struggling to oppose.

Issues of equality and justice are important. Can be particularly sensitive to how others are being treated. (May side with the "underdog.")

Often have a high need for control, which may manifest covertly or overtly.

In conflict, Middle/Outer children will tend to have a strong need to prevail. Middle/Inner children are likely to want to work things out; they may be quick to apologize and try to make things right, fearing loss of the relationship.

Challenges

May have difficulty making decisions and trusting their own point of view.

May get stuck by polarizing off another viewpoint. (In kids this may show up as rebelliousness, or a need to be in opposition.) Stubbornness is a common trait.

Drive to be humble may impede achievement: "Tooting their own horn" is not commonly in the repertoire of a Middle-Axis child who may actually diminish his or her own achievements.

May settle for mediocre when he/she could do better.

Emotion-based views may be difficult for others to understand. They can come across as too strong and be overwhelming. Or they may be seen by others as sentimental and non-objective. (And they may in fact cloud objectivity at times.)

Drive to please others may get in the way of these children meeting their own needs.

Interest in helping others may be stronger than interest in their own work.

Concrete orientation may make it difficult for this child to think abstractly.

May be loyal to a fault, maintaining a relationship or activity out of loyalty and obligation rather than a true wish to continue.

Ambivalence is common; decision-making may be difficult. Struggle typifies this axis.

Late Axis Children

Strengths/Attributes

Detail oriented.

Often verbally articulate, quick and succinct in communication.

May speak very persuasively. May be style-conscious and well dressed. Two things can confuse this when looking at children and young people: First is the influence of trends; e.g. tattered jeans may be very fashionable. Second is that young children's dress is often influenced by their parents. One clue is if the child seems "at home" in his/her stylish clothing.

Tend to be neat and meticulous.

Often popular with classmates, tending to be smooth and competent socially. May be socially outgoing.

Frequently sets the trends or subscribes to the most current trends.

Often good at setting goals and achieving them.

Conscious of others 'reaction to them and the image that they convey. (Different from the Middle-Axis's more emotional concern with others, this tends to focus on how others are viewing them).

Enjoy being "on stage" or at least are comfortable "on stage."

Often good at synthesizing information.

Tends to focus on the rational (ideas) and the material (the world of things).

In conflict, Late/Uppers in particular may prefer to keep emotions out of it and deal with the objective facts. It can be important to them that they be heard precisely. Late/lowers can have strong feeling-based responses.

Often highly competitive

Tends to focus on the finishing and refinement of the creation.

Challenges

Can be perfectionistic (sometimes rigid); feeling like a failure if they do not achieve their perceived best.

May have difficulty with depth in relationship, understanding the surface of emotions more readily.

May appear aloof.

May have trouble "taking their smile off" and receiving support or help because of their need to appear perfect and on top of things.

May be impatient with other's perceived slowness.

Competitiveness may get in the way of their trying new things. They may turn away from things that don't come easily or in which they fear they won't excel.

May be hard for these children to "loosen up" and not feel like they have to perform.

May have difficulty learning from a teacher whom they do not feel is doing his/her best.

They may write someone off whom they see as emotional or irrational.

Can have a high need to win for the sake of winning.

Focus on finishing/refinement may sometimes produce a quality "product" which reflects little originality.

In the typical school setting, Late-Axis students are often reinforced in ways that do not encourage them to appreciate or tap into other parts of themselves.

Teresa Piddington: Temperament and the Writing Process with Young Children

I recently resumed my teaching career after time away to care for my family. Upon my return to the classroom, it was important to me to teach more powerfully. I wanted to develop a more sophisticated understanding about temperament in order to differentiate and respond to the individual needs of my students. A fellow practitioner, Lyn Dillman, introduced me to some of the ways that the Creative Systems Personality Typology (CSPT) is being applied in learning environments and, as a result, I encountered promising implications for teacher learning and development.

My professional interest in personality typologies lies in appreciating and enhancing what is unique about each child while simultaneously supporting every student as they engage in the formative process of learning. The Creative Systems approach supports me in this endeavor with the way it goes beyond labels or boxes. And the fact that the foundation of Creative Systems Theory is formative processes makes it directly applicable to the tasks of the learning environment.

The CSPT enables me to understand how children with different temperaments approach learning. And it allows me to predict why, when, and how different children will excel or struggle during the various stages of a creative endeavor. To illustrate, I will focus on the activity of writing and publishing original cloth-covered books in my second grade classroom.

Early-Axis Children and the Writing Process

It is easy for Early-Axis children to excel during the early stages of the writing process (imagination, inspiration, innovation). These types of children enjoy coming up with original, elaborate ideas for their books. Their ideas stem from a personal connection to their topic of choice. Often book ideas are very large, encompassing "the whole cloth" of a topic. For example, Shane, one of my second graders, loved Yu-Gi-Oh! cards. His idea was to make an encyclopedia about his collection of 500 cards. Derrick wanted to write a fantasy about a chocolate boat that was ten miles long, held one thousand people, and could fly. Emma chose to write about her grandfather and all of his horses living on their large farm in Ohio. She also wanted to quilt her own cloth cover using scraps of fabric.

What is unique about Early-Axis children and the writing process is that they kinesthetically "know" and can "see" what they want to write about. They are able to feel, picture, and hold the whole topic in their body and in their "mind's eye." The task for me as facilitator is to appreciate the visionary capability of each child, acknowledge that I understand it to be a special gift, and provide creative freedom within a defined structure so that they can focus on and complete a written piece within my classroom's time frame.

Because Early-Axis children live in a world of innovation and imagination, the steps of editing, revision, and publication can be quite challenging for them. They know what their idea is; they've verbally told you about it; and they've also written down the main idea. For an Early, this is often enough and they're ready to move on to the next project.

At the primary school level, however, students are taught how to compose good paragraphs and to write legibly. Having to describe one part of the whole in detail is not appealing to Early-Axis children; neither is recopying sloppy text. They see these things as a waste of time and a bore, an attitude that stems from their reality of improvisation versus their finishing and polishing capabilities.

When I interpret such attitudes as Early-Axis realities, rather than as laziness, I can provide guided learning for these children during the Middle and Late stages of the writing process. For example, if I am genuinely curious about and open to the unique ideas that Earlies have and I ask them to elaborate their thoughts in complete sentences, they are willing to make the stretch. We can also talk about our common knowledge that, while rewriting a draft with correct grammar and spelling is not easy or fun for their temperament, it is, however, part of the creative process. Earlies learn that they can do it when it serves an important purpose.

Shane began the year with nearly illegible handwriting. I didn't draw attention to it because he was so excited about his ideas and his book. I did, however, spend time reviewing letter formation with my second graders. Within a few months, Shane began to notice a change in the appearance of his handwriting. He became fascinated with the fact that his letters now looked like "D'Nealian" (from the cards he so much enjoyed). With his newfound fascination for the change he observed, Shane began taking interest and pride in creating quality penmanship.

Middle-Axis Children and the Writing Process

When Middle-Axis children connect with a writing topic, they excel at the work needed to bring an idea into form (perspiration). They are dedicated and industrious writers who are able to weave together multiple resources with the intent of creating good work. They often go beyond what's expected by including numerous details and research.

Associated with their ambition is a desire to share and to be recognized for their hard work. It is imperative, therefore, that Middle-Axis children are provided with timely feedback and suitable affirmation throughout the writing process. Conferring with students one on one, pairing students for "share sessions," and allocating time for class presentations are ways through which I meet this objective.

During the Early stage of writing (inspiration) it can sometimes be difficult for Middle-Axis children to choose a topic. They may be indecisive because they have several interests, or they may want to make a choice that they think will gain their teacher's approval. The most fruitful work, however, occurs when Middle-Axis children are given time and conversation, which leads to introspection. With introspection, Middles can explore what they are most passionate about and most interested in sharing with others through their writing.

Early in the school year, when we began our first rough draft, Scott sat with his head down for quite a while. He approached me and said, "I don't know what to write about." I asked if he could name a few things that he was interested in. After some additional prompting he mentioned baseball. I spent time asking if he played on a team, what team was his favorite, whom he admired in baseball, etc. Eventually, he decided to write about a boy named Andrew who loved baseball.

At the beginning of his writing process, Scott needed to check in with me after every sentence he wrote. He needed to brainstorm for details and talk about what might come next. Slowly, with feedback and affirmation, Scott was gaining confidence. I provided him with age-appropriate readers about baseball and famous baseball players. It turned out that, in addition to Scott, several boys in the class collected baseball cards, and their families were also big fans of the game. Wonderful interactions began with his peers, and baseball became a major topic of conversation amongst the Middle-Axis boys. With interpersonal connections and conversation surrounding his greatest interest, Scott became an avid writer, planning to create a trilogy about baseball and his character Andrew.

Late-Axis Children and the Writing Process

Late-Axis children have amazing "polishing" capabilities. They live closer to completion and appearance than the other temperaments do and, therefore, are precise and deliberate when they write. Dictionaries are consulted, words are well chosen, and rough drafts often look like published manuscripts.

Understanding, appreciating, and supporting the polishing sensibilities central to Late-Axis reality goes a long way in facilitating a good learning experience.

Helping Late-Axis children see that writing is a formative process and that the finished product evolves over time reassures them that they will be happy with their final product. Sophia was excited to write a book based on the movie Charlie and the Chocolate Factory. She knew her plot and all the details that she wanted to include. At the beginning of the year however, Sophia did not have strong spelling, handwriting, or grammar skills and she refused to write. Her disruptive behavior indicated that she was still afraid of "not looking good" the first time she tried something. I spent time with her, building a stronger relationship. Step by step she began to experience that a rough draft is just a beginning and not an end. She began to feel more comfortable consulting her dictionary in front of others when she did not know how to spell a word. Her rough drafts eventually produced beautifully illustrated word-processed pages, bound in a book that was presented to parents and classmates during an "Authors 'Tea."

Late-Axis children want their careful work to be highly regarded. They can be very sensitive to criticism, and thus particular care must be taken while offering suggestions. I once made the mistake of using a pen on Kyle's rough draft. He was very upset about how the pen marks looked and about the fact that the pen couldn't be erased. We agreed that in the future I would use pencil on his drafts to indicate where capitalization, punctuation, and spelling corrections were needed.

When I am sensitive to the fact that Late-Axis children need individual emotional support and ample time to embellish their work, Lates can relax, trusting that the high standards they set for themselves will be met. Lauren was writing a book about Louisa May Alcott. She wanted her illustrations to reflect the authentic clothing and hairstyles worn by women in the 1850's. She spent time sketching several illustrations that would be suitable for her book. When she was satisfied with one, she reproduced it with meticulous detail. She also drew coordinating flower borders on every page of her book. Her attention to detail and dedication to her particular standards resulted in a remarkably informative book, much admired by both parents and peers.

In Summary

Facilitating writers' workshop is one of many joys during my teaching day. Understanding that "Earlies" need creative freedom within structure, "Middles" timely feedback and affirmation, and "Lates" ample time to embellish their work has strengthened my ability to differentiate and respond to the individual needs of my students. Comprehensive understanding of the creative process and how human beings live in and relate to its various stages is a powerful professional asset. The application of the Creative Systems Personality Typology is a particularly noteworthy part of my work with young children.

CHAPTER NINE

Advanced Reflections

The observations in this chapter may be of greatest interest to people who wish to apply the typology professionally, particularly in the healing professions. I'll expand briefly on earlier reflections about intelligence's creative multiplicity and how it relates to personality style differences. I'll take one intelligence, the intelligence of the body, and engage it with particular depth. I'll then briefly compare and contrast the CSPT with other approaches to understanding human differences. I'll touch on what the CSPT adds to common notions about psychopathology. And, finally, I'll reflect briefly on future research that could be powerful and provocative.

Intelligence's Creative Multiplicity

I've emphasized the importance of appreciating how intelligence has multiple aspects. We aren't used to thinking of intelligence as multiple. And we certainly aren't used to tying intelligence's multiplicity either to stages in creative process or personality style differences. But the role of intelligence's creative multiplicity is one of the most important recognitions if we are to understand temperament differences at all deeply.

I've noted how the recognition that one intelligence predominates with each creative stage is only a start. Each axis, in fact, draws on particular manifestations of each kind of intelligence. The chart in Figure 9-1 outlines this more complex picture. I've marked with an asterisk the intelligence that is primary with each Axis. In the other axis columns, I've then added words that describe secondary manifestations of each intelligence. Language for these multiple expressions is necessarily imprecise given that just thinking in terms of multiple intelligences can stretch how we usually think. But I've chosen words that at least point toward this essential kind of nuance.

	PRE-AXIS	EARLY-AXIS	MIDDLE-AXIS	LATE-AXIS
Body Intelligence	*The creature body, the body as nature	The body as energy, the spirit or dream body	The visceral / muscular body, the body of "heart and guts"	The physical body, the body as appearance
Imaginal Intelligence	The symbolic as a language of nature	*The symbolic as magic and inspiration	The symbolic as a language of moral order	The symbolic as fantasy and romanticism
Emotional Intelligence	Feeling as harmony and mystery	Feeling as possibility and passion	"Feeling as visceral emotion	Feeling as sentiment and pleasure
Rational Intelligence	Thought as interconnectedness	Aesthetic thought	The logic of right and wrong	*Mechanistic material thought

*Primary Organizing Intelligence

Fig. 9-1. Multiple Manifestations of Intelligence's Creative Multiplicity

People can find this multifaceted picture easiest to grasp in relationship to Patterning in Time, but it applies just as directly to Patterning in Space notions such as with the typology. For example, we've seen how imaginal intelligence is primary in the personalities of Earlies, coming alive in their creative flair. But we also find imaginal intelligence expressed with Middle-Axis personalities in the way moral, religious, and even political views can be felt with almost mythic conviction. With Lates, imaginal intelligence tends to take expression more with the romantic, or with Disneyland-style fantasy.

In another way, we see how Patterning in Time and Patterning in Space concepts interrelate—and not just conceptually, but in terms of how distinctions manifest. The way people with various personality styles experience different intelligences will be a product of all the various Patterning in Time and Patterning in Space variables that inform their lives.

The Power of Body Intelligence as a Lever for Understanding

I've observed that the typology is unusual for the attention it gives to the intelligence of the body. I've also noted that engaging body intelligence at all deeply can present particular difficulties. In our time, we aren't used to thinking of the body as anything but anatomy and physiology.

Reflections on body intelligence and its relationship to temperament brings us close to one of life's most intriguing questions: Just what is a body? On the surface, the question might seem simple to answer. We need only look down; there it is. In fact, the question is not at all simple.

Certainly it is perplexing philosophically. The body is at once something we have and something we are—not an easy fact to reconcile. And the question increasingly confronts us as we consider the body scientifically and medically. We are used to inquiring about how neurons work, about the biochemistry of digestion, or about the role of genes in disease. More and more we are recognizing that we have only begun to understand the body's rich and often very individual systemic complexity, to appreciate the body as "somebody."

A couple ways of thinking about the body that I've at least implied help fill out understanding. The first is the basic recognition that we can think of the body as intelligence. The previous chart outlines how bodily intelligence (like every other intelligence) along with being primary at a particular creative stage, makes a more limited contribution with each other stage.

Drawing on cultural-scale Patterning in Time associations helps clarify this larger picture as it applies to temperament. In the chart, I refer to the Early-Axis body as "The body as energy." Referencing Patterning in Time, this aspect of body intelligence is often described culturally in the language of spiritual essences, as with the acupuncture meridians of traditional Chinese medicine or the chakras of India's yogic traditions. With regard to temperament, I've observed how Earlies tend to move with particular ease and flexibility. They also tend to experience their bodies in terms of energy and flows.

The chart refers to the Middle-Axis body as the "visceral/muscular body." This works pretty well for both Patterning in Time and Patterning in Space distinctions. With Midde-Axis times in the West, the body was described as interplays of emotion-laden fluids—blood, phlegm, yellow bile, black bile. (Here lie the roots of words like "bilious" and "phlegmatic.") With Middle-Axis personalities, the word "visceral" makes most direct reference to the emotional, but I've added the phrase "heart and guts" to help make clear that this aspect of experience is also rooted in the body.

The chart refers to the Late-Axis body as the "physical body." With regard to the story of culture, this is the body of anatomy and physiology, the Modern Age's body as great machine. With temperament, Lates are the most likely to think of the body's workings in purely physical terms, whether in the doctor's office or at the gym. It is also Lates who tend to give greatest attention to the body's physical appearance.

The second way of approaching who we are as bodies turns to the fact that at different times and places experience organizes in the body in characteristic ways. In Chapter One, I described how formative processes manifest as a predictable sequence of polar relationships. I've also introduced each temperament-specific chapter with an image of the polar juxtaposition that most orders the reality of that particular personality axis. It is important to

THE CREATIVE SYSTEMS PERSONALITY TYPOLOGY 147

recognize that these images are more than just abstract representations. They reflect how polarity manifests in the human body.

We see this generative picture with both Patterning in Time and Patterning in Space. And we find it taking expression with both horizontal and vertical dynamics. Figure 9-2 depicts how horizontal polarity takes expression differently depending on when we find it. Inner aspects of experience get greater emphasis early on, while Outer sensibilities later come to have the greater influence. As we move from Pre-Axis to Early-Axis to Middle-Axis to Late-Axis, embodied experience moves gradually from the vicinity of the body's core toward the body's more surface layers.

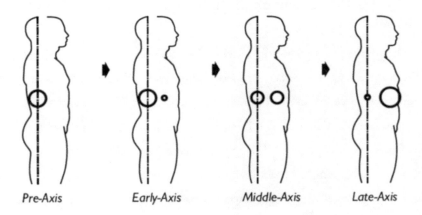

Fig. 9-2. The Evolution of Horizontal Polarity[1]

Figure 9-3 adds vertical polarity to the representation. It depicts how horizontal and vertical polarity together generate our felt experience of ourselves and how we perceive our worlds.[2]

---

1 I've noted how CST uses the terms Inner and Outer rather than the more familiar words "introvert" and "extrovert" when addressing personality style differences. The diagram helps clarify why more differentiated language is important. It follows from the creative organization of temperament that even the most Outer of Earlies will often be more Inner than most Lates, and conversely.

2 The diagrams in Figures 9-2 and 9-3 were each first presented in my book, The Creative Imperative (1984).

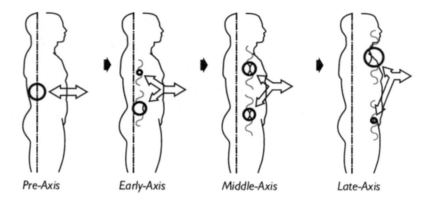

Pre-Axis   Early-Axis   Middle-Axis   Late-Axis

Fig. 9-3. The Evolution of Horizontal and Vertical Polarity[3]

The important recognition for this book's reflections is that the mapping in the diagrams applies directly to personality style differences. It describes the different ways we live in our bodies as a function of temperament.

For example, I've observed how Earlies tend most to identify with the less visible aspects of experience. It is not unusual for an Early to equate truth with some "core" of being. The fact that an Early might experience truth in this way can be a trap as well as a gift. It is what makes Earlies particularly vulnerable to Unity Fallacies. But an appreciation for how Earlies live in their bodies helps make understandable why they might see things as they do.

---

3   People often responded with confusion when I first referred to "vertical" and "horizontal" dynamics. I responded by being confused that they might be confused. I couldn't think of any way to be more concrete. Since then, I have come to appreciate how my personality style means that body intelligence observations are going to be easier for me than they are for most people. Inner and Outer seem easiest for people to grasp. Sometimes we experience more from the innermost parts of ourselves; at other times more from the body's surface. In a related way, we encounter more vertical polar dynamics bodily with how one person may seem more Upper, more in his head; while another person acts in ways that are more Lower, more from the gut. To illustrate vertical dynamics when working with a group, I will often line people up from those whose temperaments are most Upper to those whose temperaments are most Lower and then simply walk down the line, pointing my finger at the center of balance of each person's body.

I've observed that the reality of Middles has its origins in a near equal balance of polar opposites. The diagrams illustrate how this isometric relationship manifests both vertically and horizontally. They also clarify how each pole situates in the visceral and muscular regions of the body. You can think of all the qualities that I've described as characteristically Middle as following directly from this particular kind of bodily organization.

The diagrams similarly help clarify observations I've made with regard to Late-Axis sensibilities. I've noted that, of all temperaments, Lates tend to carry excitation closest to the body surface—what gives them their advantage when it comes to projecting and being visible. And I've also observed that the distance between poles is greatest with Late-Axis personality styles, something we can directly see in the diagrams. I've also cautioned against confusing Late-Axis with superficiality. The diagrams help us recognize how Late-Axis is solidly embodied, just closer to the body surface.

This more nuanced picture of the life of the body takes us beyond how most people think. But it points towards a kind of understanding that should become increasingly important. A more conscious connection with body experiences is one of the gifts that comes with Cultural Maturity's changes. A more complete relationship to body intelligence is key to how Integrative Meta-perspective provides the more complete and systemic kind of understanding needed to progress effectively as a species.

Other Temperament Approaches

Any approach to understanding human differences will help us better understand both ourselves and others. We've seen a variety of popular notions of late that claim to distinguish personality styles, relationship styles, or work styles. In most cases observations are superficial at best, but often they can still be of value. The claim that people have different "love languages," for example, while cringingly simplistic, at least helps us begin to reflect on a kind of difference.[4]

Today we also see more serious efforts. We can find attention given to "learning styles" in schools of education. Academic research often draws on the International Personality Item Pool Test. (The test gives respondents scores on five different personality traits—extroversion, agreeableness, conscientiousness, neuroticism, and openness to experience.)[5] The Myers-Briggs Type Indicator, based on the thinking of Swiss psychiatrist Carl Jung, attempts to probe underlying personality tendencies.[6] And the Diagnostic and Statistical Manual of Mental Disorders (DSM), published by the American Psychiatric Association, has a generally accepted role in psychology and psychiatry.

The important recognition for these reflections is that in each case the Creative Systems Personality Typology takes us beyond other frameworks. And it does so in ways that have direct pertinence for our time. These claims deserve elaboration.

Of particular importance is how the typology engages experience with greater depth. I've tied this to how the CSPT draws consciously on the whole of human intelligence. To a degree not found with other approaches, the typology helps us make distinctions that apply to multiple levels of human experience and interaction—how people find meaning, beliefs people may hold, how people organize experience in their bodies, the kinds of symbols and

---

4   Gary Chapman, *The Five Love Languages: How to Express Heartfelt Commitment to Your Mate*, 1992, Northfield Publishing.

5   The International Personality Item Pool (IPIP) is a public domain collection of items for use in personality tests. It is managed by the Oregon Research Institute.

6   The MBTI was constructed by Katharine Cook Briggs and her daughter Isabel Briggs Myers after being inspired by Jung's book Psychological Types, first published in 1921 (German), translated into English in 1923 as Volume 6 of The Collected Works of C.G.Jung, now: C.G. Jung, Psychological Types (The collected works of C. G. Jung, Volume 6, 3rd ed.), Princeton University Press, 1971.

metaphors a person is likely to draw on, and how people approach the forming of relationships.

Related is the way the typology is more comprehensive than most other approaches in the personality patterns that it addresses. Most psychological systems describe temperament differences primarily in behavioral terms. But for many personality styles—for example, those for which bodily intelligence or imaginal intelligence is primary—this misses what most defines a person's experience. One result is that temperament approaches are often much better at recognizing certain personality style realities than others. The CSPT presents a particularly encompassing, and arguably complete, picture of temperament diversity.

A further contribution is especially important for its clinical implications. The typology addresses differences in both style and capability and does this in an integrated way. Models of personality difference tend to be one of two types. "Pathology models" focus on capability, or lack thereof. They view difference as disease—deviation from a healthy norm. Other approaches focus on variations in style and perspective. These view difference from an egalitarian—"different strokes for different folks" perspective. Each view provides a limited half-picture. The CSPT provides an approach to understanding that helps us better appreciate both limitations and particular gifts.

That fact that the typology is not just comprehensive, but dynamically based, framed in terms of underlying processes, also makes it unusual and of particular significance. Psychological systems that are at all comprehensive tend to be empirical, "crazy quilt" collections of syndromes (eg. DSM); or largely descriptive (thinking vs feeling, etc.). Learning style approaches are again largely descriptive. Creative Systems Personality Typology distinctions are based on how people most fundamentally organize experience. Because the typology's approach is rooted in an understanding of temperaments' underpinnings, the system itself confers valuable information—what might be most helpful in a person's growth, how a person might be expected to react if stressed beyond his or her Capacitance, or how someone might tend to relate to a person of a different personality style group.

The way that the CSPT is part of Creative Systems Theory's larger framework of ideas about how human experience as a whole is patterned makes its contribution unique. The typology can address concerns like how a particular personality style would be expected to manifest differently at particular stages in an individual's life, the ways personality styles might look different in different cultural contexts, and the unique challenges and contributions we would expect to see for each personality style in these times of dramatic cultural change.

Finally, there is the broader sense in which the CSPT ties directly to the kinds of questions our human future now presents. Creative Systems Theory describes how the general kind of self-awareness that the CSPT reflects (what I've called Integrative Meta-perspective) will be increasingly important to a deep sense of identity and purpose. It also describes how the more systemic picture made possible from such perspective—and supported by collaboration between people with different temperaments—will be essential to addressing most any of the key challenges before us as a species.

More Traditional Diagnostics

I'm often asked how the perspective offered by the CSPT relates to traditional notions of psychopathology—what historically practitioners have spoken of in the language of neuroses, personality disorders, addiction patterns, and psychoses. In each case a creative frame provides at least limited insight. With each, the implications are somewhat different.

We can capture the larger portion of what psychologists might refer to as neuroses and personality disorders with the basic CSPT concepts of Axis, Pole, Aspect, Capacitance, and Symptoms. Most afflictions we encounter in everyday life can be quite adequately described in such terms. We can understand them in terms of particular personality styles and how different styles predictably respond when confronted with significant challenges to Capacitance.

The way Creative Systems Theory reframes the significance of symptoms has particular importance for how we think about many such patterns. Symptoms, as I have described them, can be thought of alternatively as bad, good, or, in a more general way, simply as information. They are evidence of a discrepancy between the Capacitance that a system has available and the Capacitance that a situation requires (if not "bad," then certainly an indication of deficiency). They represent important ways systems protect themselves ("good"). And they point toward a place where growth in a system may be possible and timely ("information" and, perhaps, information of value).

The typology is of less value where an affliction appears to span across the axes. In my experience, this is the case, for example with diagnoses such as attention-deficit/hyperactivity disorder (ADHD), autism, and obsessive-compulsive disorder (OCD). Some people today prefer to view such patterns less as pathology than as examples of non-typical neurological functioning. But at the very least, in their extreme forms, these afflictions result in very real suffering.

A place where the typology can provide some insight with such diagnoses concerns how their expanded use can result in unhelpful and inaccurate conclusions. The diagnosis of autism provides a good example. Autism disorder is a cause of major suffering, and the fact that we are better appreciating its various forms represents important advancement. But as we expand the definition and start thinking in terms of a wide spectrum of manifestations, we too easily include people who do not really belong there. Earlies can often suffer this fate. This situation is not helpful for those who actually have autism or for the Earlies who inappropriately end up with an "autism spectrum" diagnosis. We can find a related kind of confusion with the diagnosis of obsessive-compulsive disorder and Late-Axis dynamics. We see the typology's value in these contexts in the simple recognition that a solid sense of what it means to be an Early or a Late will make such confusion much less likely.

I noted previously that observations about the kinds of mind- and emotion-altering substances people of different temperaments can find attractive have application to understanding addiction. In addictive patterns, some artificial substitute for real fulfillment masquerades as the real thing. The imposter succeeds at "taking us in" because, in contrast to real fulfillment, it requires no vulnerability on our part. Depending on a person's temperament, the most attractive kind of artificial substitute can vary significantly.

It is with Early/Lowers that we most commonly find opioid addiction, though addiction to alcohol can also be a significant risk. Earlies more generally can be particularly vulnerable to having unhealthy relationships with hallucinogens and to the addicting affects of digital technologies, especially video games. Middles are most vulnerable to substances and practices that affect them at a more emotional level. That includes uppers and downers, and in particular alcohol. The great majority of people who become addicted to gambling are also Middles. Addiction with Lates is often less to physical substances than to attention or things. We see this reflected in how easily Late/Lowers in particular become addicted to social media. More specifically with regard to substance abuse, certain Lates can be attracted to diet pills or cocaine. Where we find alcohol abuse in Lates, the substance of choice will involve wine or spirits more commonly than with other temperaments.

While Creative Systems Theory provides only very limited insight into the more severe psychopathologies of psychosis, here too it makes some contribution. As a start, it draws attention to ways that underlying dynamics may be related. Psychiatry and psychology are increasingly appreciating how such patterns may have more in common than we have previously thought.

Creative Systems Theory helps us appreciate how this interplay might work. The common theme is that in some way the system loses its ability to structure creatively and collapses into various forms of protective disorganization.

I've observed that the CSPT frames Pre-Axial patterns differently than other temperament dynamics. With rare exception, in modern times we do not see such patterns as the primary influences in the personality structures of healthy individuals. (People whose cultural heritage is Pre-Axial will today tend to engage the world more as Early/Lowers or even Middle/Lowers.) With psychotic patterns, we find what are, in effect, extreme Pre-Axial dynamics struggling in a modern context. We see a collapse into the most unformed parts of formative process. This most often happens in response to some kind of marked disturbance—a significant biochemical defect, an extremely unhealthy childhood environment, or a major traumatic life event. These disturbances act at formative processes' most germinal substages to inhibit the person's capacity to manifest. Such mechanisms can intercede in the workings of any axis.

This observation helps link what people have previously tended to think of as separate phenomena. We see such Pre-Axial-like mechanisms with psychoses of all sorts. The effect appears to happen earliest in formative process with organic psychoses, where the symptoms are a result of direct tissue damage, internal toxicity, or an external pharmacologic agent. Here we find the greatest disorganization. In schizophrenic patterns (thought disorders), the effect seems to be somewhat later, and with the affective psychoses (severe manias and depressions) somewhat later still. With each of these kinds of patterns there is some beginning establishment of structure, but not yet of sufficient substance to handle major engagements with reality. The fact that such patterns often blend and overlap is easily understandable within this framework.

This way of framing psychosis can also help us better understand characteristic symptomology. For example, schizophrenic symptoms can be thought of in terms of two counterbalancing dynamics. First, they express the Pre-Axial unformedness of the system. We commonly see symptoms such as hallucinations (the taking of inner reality for external fact), loose associations (a lack of organization in thought), delusions (commonly reflecting a loss of boundary distinction, as for example, with the belief that a person on television is talking specifically to you), and withdrawal (from the world of things). At the same time, symptoms represent a particular kind of structure, a making of form from what is available within that diminished reality. In an important sense, psychosis is not so much a disintegration of the psyche as an attempt to salvage it. Those loose associations make very effective boundaries. Delusions function to create unique identity and, along with hallucinations, provide a safe sense of connection and communication with the world. The common bodily disorganization in chronic patterns, in which the different body parts can seem fragmented, reflects each of these complementary mechanisms; being a kind of disruption and yet a very effective way to keep the whole from merging into unity.

Bringing a creative frame to understanding psychosis also helps with common controversies regarding etiology. Psychotic patterns clearly indicate that something is wrong or broken, but the causes can be complex and open to debate. The best of thinking today tends to include both genetic and environmental factors. The application of a creative frame doesn't reconcile disagreements over whether particular psychotic patterns result from biochemical defects or are a product of aberrant childhood experiences. But it does offer that we might think in more than either/or terms. Many things can serve to disrupt the germinal substages of formative process. Environmentally, the cause could be a family matrix in which primary bonding is disrupted or, alternatively, where little if any individual identity is tolerated within the system. Biochemically there could be a genetic defect, affecting either the general capacity for rhythmic progression or the child's specific ability to establish that early bond.at I think of the various psychotic patterns as "final common pathways" for a multiplicity of often interwoven etiological processes.

Possible Future Research

Only a very limited amount of formal research has been done with the typology. With my other life demands, it is not where I have chosen to put my attention. And, given the fact that simple diagnostic tests are not terribly useful when applying the typology, such research is not as easily done as one might wish.[7] But there is much in the way of formal research that could serve to further fill out the typology and its implications. Especially with today's growing sophistication in the use of imaging technologies, a variety of potentially powerful and provocative experiments become possible.

Certainly of interest would be the use of imaging to confirm cognitive differences between axial patterns, and affirm observations about pattern-related capacities. So would the use of such approaches to more directly address underlying mechanisms. I would have particular interest in seeing if imaging techniques could confirm the link between Patterning in Time and Patterning in Space observations. Support for the thesis that we find related cognitive patterns with parallel stages in personal and cultural development, and also with temperament, would provide important confirmation of Creative Systems Theory's contribution in the history of ideas.

---

[7] Wholly different CSPT temperaments may give the same answer on diagnostic tests.

AFTERWORD

A Most Timely Significance

We are all better temperament diagnosticians than we realize. We choose our friends and our partners in ways that make clear that at some level we recognize personality style differences. And I've described how we all use terms when speaking of others that are, in effect, diagnostic for such differences, such as quirky, steadfast, or stylish. I've proposed an explanation for why in times past the kind of perspective we have examined in these pages has not been obvious. And I've suggested that in the future we should expect this to change. If you have gotten this far, you should now have a good beginning sense of the Creative Systems Personality Typology and how you might apply it.

The typology is one of the aspects of Creative Systems Theory for which people through the years have most often expressed gratitude. I have been pleased to see how useful people have found its observations and how readily they have often been able to put them into practice. And that includes not just professionals in spheres like psychology and education, where the typology's contribution is most obviously applicable; but also people addressing questions of identity and relationships from all walks of life and of all ages. It has often been great fun.

When it comes to the typology's significance, of particular importance for me has been its relationship to the tasks of Cultural Maturity. I've described how the ability to bring systemic perspective to the ways we understand and how we make decisions is a defining characteristic of culturally mature understanding. That the CSPT is able to bring such nuance to understanding who we are and what makes us similar and different gives it an essential place in this needed new picture. And the way that it supports the deeply collaborative kinds of engagement that questions of all sorts increasingly require gives its contribution particular importance for our time.

I've also noted a more ultimate, conceptual kind of significance. The fact that Creative Systems Theory's application of a creative frame makes possible both nuanced development distinctions and the CSPT's detailed here-and-now kinds of contextual distinctions is at the least a striking accomplishment. And the fact that the theory helps us appreciate how such observations are related and brings them together as part of a larger integrated perspective supports the theory's importance in the larger evolution of human understanding.

Whether your particular interest with the typology has been more personal, more professional, or more conceptual, I hope you've found this book's reflections of value. My fascination with what the typology has to teach has only increased over the course of my life.

APPENDIX

Creative Systems Theory and the Concept of Cultural Maturity

Many readers will appreciate more of an introduction to Creative Systems Theory and the concept of Cultural Maturity. In the piece that follows, I provide additional background. I've touched briefly on many of its main observations in describing the basis for the typology. Think of these reflections as adding flesh to previous bare-boned conceptual observations. You can find a more extended introduction in the book *Insight: Creative Systems Theory's Radical New Picture of Human Possibility*.[1]

Background

Creative Systems Theory had its beginnings in attempts to better understand the workings of creative process. In time it evolved into an overarching framework for understanding purpose, change, and interrelationship in human systems. The theory has its foundation in the recognition that our meaning-making, toolmaking—we could say simply "creative"—nature is what ultimately defines us.

Creative Systems Theory concepts help us step back and appreciate culture's larger story, how human understanding has evolved over time. That includes not only the evolution of belief, but also the changing cognitive structures that have produced those beliefs. And specifically it includes changes

---

[1] Charles M. Johnston, MD, *Insight: Creative Systems Theory's Radical New Picture of Creative Possibility*, 2022, ICD Press.

that reorder understanding in our time. The theory's comprehensive framework offers a way to replace Modern Age mechanistic thinking with ideas that better reflect that we are alive, and alive in the particular way that makes us human.

The concept of Cultural Maturity follows from Creative Systems Theory's larger picture. Much of my life's work has involved attempting to make sense of critical challenges ahead for the species. My focus had been less on technical challenges than on human challenges. Central to these efforts has been the observation that effectively addressing many of the most important of these challenges will require new kinds of human abilities. That observation shifted from an obstacle to something more consistent with hope, when I recognized that at least the potential for these new abilities was built into who we are. We don't have to invent them from whole cloth. The Creative Systems concept of Cultural Maturity describes the core task of our time as a new—and newly possible—"growing up" as a species.[2] Cultural Maturity involves changes not just in what we think, but how we think. These changes make essential new abilities possible. They also make possible new ways of thinking, such as Creative Systems Theory.

My efforts over the years have approached the ideas of Creative Systems Theory and the concept of Cultural Maturity from multiple directions. I've endeavored to clarify their essential roles in helping us address questions ahead in all parts of our lives—from the challenges of effective leadership and governance to what love and human relationship more generally will require of us. With my direction of the Institute for Creative Development (a Seattle-based think tank and center for advanced leadership training), I worked for

---

2   I first introduced Creative Systems Theory and the concept of Cultural Maturity with my 1984 book The Creative Imperative: Human Growth and Planetary Evolution (Celestial Arts). The book Creative Systems Theory: A Comprehensive Theory of Purpose, Change, and Interrelationship in Human Systems (2021, ICD Press) provides the most detailed description of the theory.

twenty-five years to teach about and foster culturally mature leadership. And I've written over a dozen books and numerous articles that in various ways expand on the ideas of Creative Systems Theory and the broader implications of culturally mature understanding.

Here I will touch briefly on the shift in perspective that Creative Systems Theory represents. I will then turn more specifically to the concept of Cultural Maturity and examine some of the new human capacities Cultural Maturity's changes make possible. I will take a closer look at some of Creative Systems Theory's more detailed formulations. And, in concluding, I will give some particular attention to the implications of these notions for the tasks of future leadership and summarize the evidence that what I have described is correct.

The Power of a Creative Frame

The insight that makes Creative Systems Theory's more detailed formulations wholly new is the power of a creative frame. Thinking in creative terms provides a new Fundamental Organizing Concept able to take us beyond machine model notions of times past. In a related way, the application of a creative frame transcends past romantic and idealist objections to mechanistic notions. We can think of a creative frame as following directly from Cultural Maturity's cognitive reordering.

Creative Systems Theory includes three basic kinds of "patterning concepts," notions that help us think about truth in ways that better reflect that we are living beings. Each kind of patterning concept has its foundation in a creative reframing of cognition. Patterning in Time concepts concern truth's temporal relativity. They address change processes in human systems—the dynamics of innovation, individual development, the growth of relationships, and, of particular importance, the evolution of culture. Patterning in Space notions address here-and-now contextual relativity. We can use them to help make sense of inner psychological dynamics as well as the workings of larger systems, from families and organizations to nations. The Creative Systems Personality Typology is the most fully developed Patterning in Space tool. The third group of notions, what the theory calls Whole-Person/Whole-System patterning concepts, address more general questions of possibility, motivation, and capacity.

Cultural Maturity

The Creative Systems Theory concept of Cultural Maturity focuses more specifically on today. It presents a new guiding narrative able to replace Modern Age assumptions that today, more and more, fail to serve us. It also describes new kinds of skills and capacities that will be needed if we are to effectively make our way. And it delineates how the task involves not just thinking new things, but thinking in new, more complete and systemic ways. We can think of culturally mature perspective as providing the future's needed "new common sense." Creative Systems Theory's overarching formulations reflect this more mature and complete kind of perspective.

The concept of Cultural Maturity is not as easy a notion as the simple phrase "growing up" might suggest. For most people, it challenges favorite assumptions. And it requires us to think in more encompassing ways than we are used to. But where it takes us is ultimately straightforward. I find it helpful to think of the changes that produce culturally mature understanding in a couple of steps. In the end, these steps reflect aspects of a single mechanism, but looking at them separately assists us in getting started.

The first change process gives the concept its name. Cultural Maturity brings a new, more mature relationship between culture and the individual. In times past, culture has functioned as a parent in the lives of individuals, providing us with clear rules to live by. These cultural absolutes worked to offer a sense of shared identity and connectedness with others. They also protected us from life's very real uncertainties and immense complexities.

Today, this traditional relationship is changing. Cultural absolutes are serving us less and less well. They are also having diminishing influence. This loss of past collective rules has Janus-faced implications. It can reveal possibilities that before now we could not have considered. But at the same time, it can bring a disturbing sense of absence. Clearly something more is needed. If all that we are seeing today is a loss of past parental guideposts, we have problems. New possibility would be only of the postmodern, anything-goes, everybody-gets-their-own-truth, sort. What might seem to be freedom would produce instead only a loss of order and a dangerous kind of aimlessness.

The second kind of change process is what makes today's loss of past absolutes anything to celebrate. Cultural Maturity is not just about acting in more grown-up ways. It involves developmentally predicted cognitive changes. It turns out that the same change mechanisms that generate today's loss of past truths also create the potential for new, more mature ways of understanding. One way to think of culturally mature thought is that it is post-postmodern.

Creative Systems Theory uses an ungainly (but quite precise) term for the cognitive reordering that gives us Cultural Maturity and its new vantage for understanding: Integrative Meta-perspective. Integrative Meta-perspective involves, first, a more complete kind of stepping back from our complex natures. This stepping back creates greater awareness. It is also what creates new distance from culture's past parental role. And at the same time, Cultural Maturity's cognitive changes involve a new and deeper kind of engagement with the whole of our cognitive complexity, all the diverse aspects of who we are. The result is not just further abstraction, but the more fully embodied kind of understanding that is needed for mature decision-making.[3]

---

3   The book Rethinking How We Think: Integrative Meta-Perspective and the Cognitive "Growing Up" On Which Our Future Depends (2020, ICD Press) provides a detailed examination of this cognitive reordering.

We will come back shortly for a closer look. For now, it is enough to appreciate that Integrative Meta-perspective, by allowing us to both more fully step back from and more deeply engage the whole of how we understand, lets us think in ways that are more encompassing and complete than was possible in times past. We could say that this new way of thinking is more systemic—or simply more wise. I often use the metaphor of a box of crayons. The crayons represent systemic aspects. The box represents more encompassing perspective. Integrative Meta-perspective lets us step back and draw more consciously—and deeply—on the whole box.

New Questions and New Human Capacities

I've proposed that addressing critical questions before us will require new kinds of human capacities. One of the best arguments for the concept of Cultural Maturity is that its cognitive changes make needed new capacities possible. Noting a few of these capacities helps affirm the importance of Culturally Maturity's changes and highlights important aspects of where they take us.

Accepting a newly ultimate kind of responsibility: As we leave behind thinking of culture as a symbolic parent, we necessarily assume a new depth of responsibility, and not just for our actions, but for the truths we draw on.

Getting beyond the us-and-them polar assumptions of times past: The importance of this further capacity is most obvious with how it helps us begin to leave behind the "chosen people/evil other" polarizations that through history have led to war. Creative Systems Theory describes how relationships of all sorts—from those between nations, to those that define leadership, to those we find with friendship or love—have always before been based on projection. We've related not as whole beings, but as symbolic halves that together made a whole. The theory also describes how Integrative Meta-perspective's more systemic vantage helps us re-own the projections that before have produced mythologized perceptions of both the demonized and idealized sort. With Cultural Maturity's cognitive reordering, we become better able to act in the world as whole systems, and to engage other systems as whole systems.

Better appreciating the fact of limits: The Modern Age story was heroic: We celebrated a world without limits. Increasingly, however, we recognize that if we are not more attentive to real limits, we are doomed. Integrative Meta-perspective's more encompassing vantage makes clear that, whatever our concern, in the end limits come with the territory. The greater maturity that comes with Integrative Meta-perspective applies to real limits of every sort—limits to what we can do (as with environmental limits), limits to what we can know and predict (as we recognize with good risk assessment), and limits to what we can be for one another (as with culturally mature relationships of all sorts). It also reveals how a mature acknowledgement of limits, rather than limiting us, in the end increases possibility.

Learning to better tolerate complexity and uncertainty: Today, questions of every kind confront us with new complexities and uncertainties. Because Integrative Meta-perspective draws directly on our own systemic complexity, it helps us make sense of and tolerate complexity in the world around us. And for a related reason, Cultural Maturity's changes make us more comfortable in uncertainty's presence. Creative Systems Theory describes how ideas become ideological—and thus expressions of last-word truth—when we make one aspect of a larger complexity (one crayon in that systemic box) the whole of understanding. When we engage understanding more fully, uncertainty becomes intrinsic to any deep understanding of truth. Creative Systems Theory goes further to describe how both complexity and uncertainty are necessary ingredients in cognition's "creative" workings.

Learning to think about what matters in more systemically complete ways: With Integrative Meta-perspective we become able to "measure" significance in ways that better reflect the whole of who we are and the whole of anything we might wish to consider. For example, moral decisions become less about choosing between good and evil than about acknowledging competing goods and discerning where the most life-affirming choices ultimately lie. And as relationships of all sorts require us to step beyond two-halves-make-a-whole projective dynamics, in a similar way, Integrative Meta-perspective lets us more directly discern when a human connection enhances life. This new capacity applies most broadly to the critical task of rethinking advancement. Our times demand that we think about wealth and progress in ways that are more encompassing and complete.

Better understanding how events happen in a context, particularly in the context of our time in culture's story: Thinking that serves us going forward must help us make more dynamic and nuanced kinds of discernments. Of particular importance, it must help us be more attentive to context. With culturally mature truth, the "when" and the "where" are always as important as the "what." Such contextual relativity is wholly different from relativity of the postmodern, anything-goes sort. Culturally mature understanding allows us to make highly precise distinctions that are precise exactly because they take contextual nuances into account. We can think of Creative Systems Theory's framework for understanding purpose, change, and interrelationship in human systems as a set of tools for making such context-specific observations. The Creative Systems Personality Typology is a specific example of this kind of contribution.

Integrative Meta-perspective and Polarity

A closer look at the cognitive reorganization that underlies Cultural Maturity's changes helps us appreciate why such new capacities result, and also ties them more directly to Creative Systems Theory's conceptual framework. I've described how Integrative Meta-perspective involves at once more fully stepping back from and more deeply engaging the whole of our human complexity. Reflecting briefly on a couple of ways of thinking about that complexity—the role of polarity in how we think and the fact of intelligence's multiplicity—provides important further insight.

Let's first consider the fact of polarity. Creative Systems Theory describes how each chapter in culture's story to this point has framed truth in terms of qualities set in polar juxtaposition (for example, in modern times, mind versus body, leader versus follower, or science versus religion). Robert Frost observed that "It almost scares a man the way things come in pairs." With Cultural Maturity's cognitive reordering, we both step back from and more deeply engage past either/or relationships. In the process, we become able to appreciate them as aspects of larger systemic realities.

Creative Systems Theory brings detail to what we see. As a start, it addresses why we see polarity in the first place. After proposing that what most makes us human is our meaning-making, toolmaking, "creative" prowess, it goes on to describe how our cognitive mechanisms are designed to support this capacity for innovation. Specifically with regard to polarity, it describes how the fact that we think in polar terms follows directly from this creative picture.

Creative Systems Theory delineates how the same progression of polar relationships orders creative/formative change of all sorts—from an act of invention to the evolution of culture. Such change begins with a newly created aspect budding off from its original context. With each succeeding stage in formative process's first half, polar aspects become more separate, juxtaposing in evolving, creatively predicted ways. With the second, more mature half of any formative process, polarities reconcile to create a new and larger whole. We come to experience the newly created entity now as "second nature."

This sequence provides a template for understanding formative process wherever we might find it. Creative Systems Theory calls the generic map that results—applicable to formative dynamics from the most personal of insights to the most encompassing of collective processes—the Creative Function..

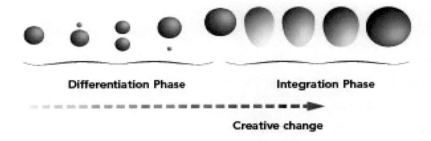

Fig. A-1. The Creative Function

We can recognize this two-part extended picture in personal psychological development. The underlying impetus with development in the first half of an individual life is toward distinction and the establishing of identity as form. With childhood we begin discovering who we are, with adolescence we make our first forays into the social world, and during adulthood we establish our unique place in that world. Second-half-of-life maturing involves more specifically integrative tasks: It is about learning how to live in the world with the greatest perspective, depth, and integrity.

When applied at a cultural scale, this picture of evolving polar relationships has critical implications for understanding the times in which we live. I've described Cultural Maturity's "growing up" in how we think and act in terms of Integrative Meta-perspective and the more encompassing kind of understanding it makes possible. Integrative Meta-perspective helps us get our minds around apparent polar opposites on the largest of scales. The Creative Function helps us appreciate how Cultural Maturity's cognitive reordering is a predicted consequence of our time in culture's evolving creative story.

We don't need Creative Systems Theory's detailed formulations to appreciate the relationship between polarity and Integrative Meta-perspective. F. Scott Fitzgerald proposed that the sign of a first-rate intelligence (we might say a mature intelligence) is the ability to hold two contradictory truths simultaneously in mind without going mad. His reference was to personal maturity, but this capacity is such an inescapable part of culturally mature perspective that we could almost say it defines it.

One of the simplest ways to think about how culturally mature perspective changes the way we understand draws on the basic observation that needed new understandings of every sort "bridge" polar assumptions of times past.[4] We can think of Cultural Maturity's point of departure as itself a "bridging" dynamic. We step back and see the relationship of culture and the individual in more encompassing terms. Cultural Maturity "bridges" ourselves and our societal contexts (or, put another way, ourselves and final truth). It is through this most fundamental "bridging" that we leave behind society's past parental function.

This most encompassing linkage holds within it a multitude of more local "bridgings." Nothing more characterized the last century's defining conceptual advances than their linking of previously unquestioned polar truths. Physics' new picture provocatively circumscribed the realities of matter and energy, space and time, object and observer. New understandings in biology more closely linked humankind with the natural world, and by reopening timeless questions about life's origins, joined the purely physical with the organic. And the ideas of modern psychology, neurology, and sociology have provided an increasingly integrated picture of the workings of conscious with unconscious, mind with body, self with society, and more.

---

4 I organized my early book Necessary Wisdom: Meeting the Challenge of a New Cultural Maturity (1991, Celestial Arts) around this basic observation.

If the relationship between "bridging" and Cultural Maturity is to make ultimately useful sense, we need to include a couple of critical distinctions. We need first to clearly distinguish between personal maturity and Cultural Maturity. The ability to hold contradictory truths that F. Scott Fitzgerald described has been a characteristic of wise thought throughout history. In contrast, none of the last century's defining insights that I just noted would have made sense before now. The "bridging" of cultural realities that the concept of Cultural Maturity describes is specifically a phenomenon of our time.

We must also avoid confusing "bridging" as I am using the term with more familiar outcomes (which is why I put the word in quotes). The result is wholly different from averaging or compromise, from walking the white line in the middle of the road. And just as fundamentally it is different from simple oneness, the collapsing of one pole into the other that we commonly see with more spiritual interpretations. "Bridging" in this sense is about consciously drawing on the whole creative box of crayons.

Cultural Maturity and Intelligence's Creative Multiplicity

Framing Cultural Maturity's cognitive reordering in terms of intelligence's multiplicity provides further nuance and helps us better put the changes that result—and their significance—in historical perspective. Creative Systems Theory highlights how intelligence has multiple parts. Besides our rationality (in which we take appropriate pride), intelligence has other aspects, some more emotional or symbolic, others more sensory.

Most of what Creative Systems Theory has to say about our diverse ways of knowing is beyond the scope of this short article,[5] but certain observations are specifically relevant. Especially pertinent is how Creative Systems Theory explains why we have multiple intelligences. The theory delineates how our various intelligences work together to support and drive our creative proclivities. We find a related intelligence-specific progression with every kind of human formative process—be it invention, individual development, the growth of a relationship, or, of particular importance for these reflections, the evolution of culture. Different aspects of intelligence and different relationships between intelligences most define experience at different creative stages.

Creative Systems Theory delineates four basic types of intelligence.

For ease of conversation, we can refer to them simply as the intelligences of the body, the imagination, the emotions, and the intellect. (The theory uses the fancier language that I include in Figure A-2.) CST proposes that these different ways of knowing represent more than merely diverse approaches to processing information. They represent the windows through which we make sense of our worlds and the formative tendencies that lead us to shape our worlds in the ways that we do.

---

[5] See Charles M. Johnston, MD, *Intelligence's Creative Multiplicity: And Its Critical Role in the Future of Understanding*, 2023, ICD Press.

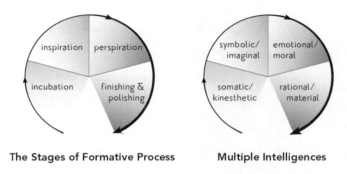

The Stages of Formative Process   Multiple Intelligences

Fig. A-2. Formative Process and Intelligence's Creative Multiplicity

This observation has major practical implications. It provides the basis for Creative Systems Theory's framework for understanding the workings of human systems. It also has consequences of a more philosophical and paradigmatic sort. I've hinted at how Creative Systems Theory is significant not only because it provides new conceptual tools for making our way, but also because it successfully takes us beyond the kind of thinking that has defined Modern Age understanding.

Enlightenment thinkers such as Sir Isaac Newton and René Descartes described reality as a great clockworks. While machine-model thinking has made a huge contribution—it has given us not only scientific and industrial advancement, but our modern concept of the individual, as well—it presents real problems if we wish to talk about living systems. There is no more significant conceptual challenge in our time than finding ways to address human systems more directly in living terms. Any culturally mature notion at least implies this important conceptual leap, but Creative Systems Theory makes it explicitly. I've proposed that the creative frame which serves as the theory's foundation represents a new Fundamental Organizing Concept that effectively takes us beyond the mechanistic assumptions of times past. By drawing on this dynamic and generative approach to understanding, the theory is able to provide highly delineated formulations that directly reflect the fact that we are living—and human—beings.

A more historical look at Integrative Meta-perspective through the lens of intelligence's multiplicity helps fill out the conceptual leap that produces culturally mature understanding. Modern Age thought similarly had its origins in a new kind of cognitive orientation. And stepping back from previous ways of knowing was a big part of it. We became better able to step back from the more mystical sensibilities that gave us the beliefs of the Middle Ages.

Along with this more general stepping back, rationality came to have a newly central significance. The rational now stood clearly separate from the subjective aspects of experience and became specifically allied with conscious awareness. The result was a new, as-if-from-a-balcony sense of clarity and objectivity. This, combined with the new belief in the individual as logical choice-maker that accompanied it, produced all the great advances of the Modern Age.

But while Modern Age thought was a grand achievement, Integrative Meta-perspective's stepping back represents a wholly different sort of accomplishment. Awareness comes to stand more fully separate from the whole of our intelligence's systemic complexity—including the rational. Integrative Meta-perspective offers that we might step back equally from aspects of ourselves that we formerly treated as objective and those that we had thought of as subjective. In the process, it offers that we might better step back from the whole of intelligence.

And there is more. Culturally mature understanding requires not only that we be aware of intelligence's multiple aspects, but also that in a whole new sense we embody each of these aspects. It directly draws on all of our diverse ways of knowing. Culturally mature understanding requires thinking in a rational sense—indeed, it expands rationality's role. But just as much it involves more directly plumbing the feeling, imagining, and sensing aspects of who we are. And this is the case as much for the most rigorous of hard theory as when our concerns are more personal. Making sense of most anything about us—the values we hold, the nature of identity, what it means to have human relationship—increasingly requires this more encompassing kind of understanding.

An important outcome when we frame Cultural Maturity in this way might at first seem contradictory. On one hand, because culturally mature perspective draws on multiple, often conflicting aspects of who we are, its conclusions are less absolute and once-and-for-all than those we are used to. I've described how they require that we be more comfortable with complexity and uncertainty. But, at the same time, we can appropriately argue that culturally mature understanding is more "objective" than what it replaces. Certainly it is more complete.

Enlightenment thought might have claimed ultimate objectivity, but this was in fact objectivity of only a limited sort. Besides leaving culture's parental status untouched, it left experience as a whole divided—objective (in the old sense) set opposed to subjective, mind set opposed to body, thoughts set opposed to feelings (and anything else that does not conform to modernity's rationalist/materialist worldview). We cannot ultimately claim to be objective if we have left out half of the evidence. Culturally mature objectivity is of a more specifically all-the-crayons-in-the-box sort.

The fact that we can understand Cultural Maturity in terms of developmentally predicted cognitive changes also points toward an important further implication suggested earlier. It supports being legitimately optimistic about what may lie ahead. If Cultural Maturity's cognitive changes are, as potential built into who we are, the likelihood that we can thrive and prosper in times ahead increases significantly. And, if this is a cognitive reordering that we can actively practice and facilitate, that likelihood increases further.[6]

Creative Systems Theory and the Application of a Creative Frame

We can arrive at a creative frame in multiple ways. As a start, we can do so by reflecting on what Integrative Meta-perspective teaches us about the workings of polarity. And we don't need the Creative Functions developmental picture to get there. I've described how culturally mature understanding "bridges" the polarized assumptions of times past. If we look closely, we recognize that polar relationships reflect an underlying symmetry. I've noted how polarities juxtapose some softer, we could say, more left hand—or to use language from psychology, more archetypally feminine—quality, with another quality that is harder, we could say, more right-hand—or more archetypally masculine. Creative Systems Theory describes how this basic symmetry is key to the workings of formative process. I've emphasized the important sense in which the relationship between the two hands of any polarity when understood systemically becomes "procreative."

We get to a similar place if we shift our attention to intelligence. I've described how Integrative Meta-perspective makes it possible to better hold the whole of human intelligence. And I've observed Creative Systems Theory's claim that intelligence's multiplicity functions to support and drive formative process. Integrative Meta-perspective, just from where it takes us, thrusts us into a world in which the workings of intelligence are dynamic and systemic, and this in a whole new sense—we could say in a sense that is expressly creative.

A closer look at intelligence's multiplicity and its role in formative process helps fill out this creative picture. It also provides a glimpse into how Creative

---

6 See Charles M Johnston, MD, Hope and the Future: Confronting Today's Crisis of Purpose, 2018, ICD Press.

Systems Patterning in Time notions help us understand change in human systems. Creative Systems Theory proposes that we are the uniquely creative creatures we are not merely because we are conscious, but because of the ways that the various aspects of our intelligence work, and in particular, how they work together. The theory describes how our various intelligences—or we might better say, "sensibilities," to reflect all that they encompass—relate in specifically creative ways. And it delineates how different ways of knowing, and different relationships between ways of knowing, predominate at specific times in any human change processes. The way Creative Systems Theory ties the underlying structures of intelligence to patterns of change in human systems both helps us better understand change and hints at the possibility of better predicting it.

The theory argues that our various intelligences work together in ways that are not merely collaborative, but specifically creative. It describes how human intelligence is uniquely configured to support creative change—to drive and facilitate its workings. Our various modes of intelligence, juxtaposed like colors on a color wheel, function together as creativity's mechanism. That wheel, like the wheel of a car or a Ferris wheel, is continually turning, continually in motion. The way the various facets of intelligence juxtapose makes change, and specifically purposeful change, inherent to our natures.

With creativity's initial" incubation" stage, the dominant intelligence is the kinesthetic, body intelligence, if you will. It is like I am pregnant, but don't yet know quite with what. What I do know takes the form of "inklings" and faint "glimmerings," inner sensings. If I want to feed this part of the creative process, I do things that help me to be reflective and to connect in my body. I take a long walk in the woods, draw a warm bath, build a fire in the fireplace.

Next comes creativity's "inspiration" stage, the stage in which new possibility first comes into the light. The dominant intelligence here is the imaginal—that which most defines art, myth, and the let's-pretend world of young children. The products of this period in the creative process may appear suddenly—Archimedes's "Eureka"—or they may come more subtly and gradually. It is this stage, and this part of our larger sensibility, that we tend to most traditionally associate with things creative.

With creativity's "perspiration" stage we give inspiration solid form. The dominant intelligence is different still, more emotional and visceral—the intelligence of heart and guts. It is here that we confront the hard work of finding the right approach and the most satisfying means of expression. We also confront limits to our skills and are challenged to push beyond them. The perspiration stage tends to bring a new moral commitment and emotional edginess. We must compassionately but unswervingly confront what we have created if it is to stand the test of time.

With creativity's "finishing and polishing" stage we give creation detail and engage the tasks of completion. Here, rational intelligence comes to have the more dominant role. This period is more conscious and more concerned with aesthetic precision than the periods previous. It is also more concerned with audience and outcome. It brings final focus to the creative work, the clarity of thought and nuances of style needed for effective communication.

While we might assume that the creative task is now done, we've, in fact, come at best half of the way. And the changes that mark formative process's second half are equally as important and transforming. With creation's second half, we step back from the work and appreciate it with new perspective. We become more able to appreciate the relationship of the work to its creative contexts: both ourselves and the time and place in which it was created. The result of this "seasoning" process is a more integrative picture. I've spoken of how the work becomes in a new sense, "second nature." Specifically with regard to intelligence, we come to use our diverse ways of knowing more consciously together. We become better able to apply our intelligences in various combinations and balances as time and situation warrant and through this process to engage the work as a whole and ourselves as a whole in relationship to it.

We can tie this progression to formative processes of all sorts. We see something similar whether our concern is an act of innovation, personal psychological development, or culture and its evolution. For example, we find the same bodily intelligence that orders creative "incubation" playing a particularly prominent role in the infant's rhythmic world of movement, touch, and taste. The realities of early tribal cultures also draw deeply on body sensibilities. Truth in tribal societies is synonymous with the rhythms of nature and, through dance, song, story, and drumbeat, with the body of the tribe.

We find the same imaginal intelligence that we saw ordering creative "inspiration" taking prominence in the play-centered world of the young child. We also hear it voiced with particular strength in early civilizations—such as ancient Greece or Egypt, the Incas and Aztecs in the Americas, or the classical East—with their mythic pantheons and great symbolic tales.

We find the same emotional and moral intelligence that orders creative "perspiration" occupying center stage in adolescence, with its deepening passions and pivotal struggles for identity. It can also be felt with particular strength in the beliefs and values of the European Middle Ages, times marked by feudal struggle and ardent moral conviction (and, today, where struggle and conflict seem to be forever recurring).

In a similar way, we find the same rational intelligence that comes forward for the "finishing and polishing" tasks of creativity taking new prominence in young adulthood, as we strive to create our unique place in the world of adult expectations. This more refined and refining aspect of intelligence stepped to the fore culturally during the Renaissance and the Age of Reason and, in the West, has held sway into modern times.

Finally, and of particular pertinence to the concept of Cultural Maturity, we find the same, more consciously integrative relationship to intelligence that we see in the "seasoning" stage of a creative act ordering the unique developmental capacities—the wisdom—of a lifetime's second half. We can also see this same, more integrative relationship with intelligence just beneath the surface in our current cultural stage in the Western advances that have transformed understanding through the last century.

We associate the Age of Reason with Descartes's assertion that "I think, therefore I am." We could make a parallel assertion for each of these other cultural stages: "I am embodied, therefore I am"; "I imagine, therefore I am"; "I am a moral being, therefore I am"; and, if the concept of Cultural Maturity is accurate, "I understand maturely and systemically—with the whole of myself—therefore I am." The concept of Cultural Maturity proposes that the words you have just read about intelligence's creative workings have made sense because such consciously integrative dynamics are beginning to reorder how we think and perceive.

Creative Systems Theory Patterning Concepts

I've observed how Creative Systems Theory includes three basic kinds of "patterning concepts." Patterning in Time concepts address change in human systems. The chart in Figure A-3 summarizes Creative Systems Theory Patterning in Time observations as they pertain to common developmental processes—a simple creative act, individual human development, the growth of a relationship, and, of particular importance, the history of culture. It also adds the language that the theory uses in making such distinctions: Pre-Axis for "incubation stage" sensibilities, Early-Axis for "inspiration stage" sensibilities,

Middle-Axis for "perspiration stage" sensibilities, and Late-Axis for "finishing and polishing" stage sensibilities.

			CREATIVE STAGES			
Pre-Axis	Early-Axis	Middle-Axis	Late-Axis	Transition	Integrative Stages	
			MAJOR PERIODICITIES			
A CREATIVE EVENT						
Incubation	Inspiration	Perspiration	Finishing & Polishing	Presentation	Becoming "Second Nature" (Integration of the newly created form into self and culture)	
A LIFETIME						
Prenatal Period & Infancy	Childhood	Adolescence	Early Adulthood	Midlife Transition	Mature Adulthood (From knowledge to wisdom—integration of self as formed identity with the ground of being)	
A RELATIONSHIP						
Pre-relationship	Falling in Love	Time of Struggle	Established Relationship	Time of Questioning	Mature Intimacy (Relationship as two whole people—marriage of the "loved" and the "lover" within each person)	
THE HISTORY OF CULTURE						
Pre-History	Golden Ages	Middle Ages	Age of Reason	Transitional Culture	Cultural Maturity (Larger meeting of the form and context of culture)	

Fig. A-3. Formative Process from the Perspective of Creative Systems Theory.

Patterning in Space notions address here-and-now systemic differences. The Creative Systems Personality Typology is the most filled out and recognized Patterning in Space tool. But we can also use Patterning in Space notions to help tease apart internal psychological mechanisms and to map the dynamics and interactions of interpersonal relationships, organizations, communities, nations, and the planet as a whole.

The third kind of patterning notions, what the theory calls Whole-Person/Whole-System patterning concepts, address attributes that are products of systems as entireties. They address what truth at its most basic becomes with Culture Maturity's cognitive reordering. Some examples include the concept of Aliveness, a general way of talking about possibility and motivation; the idea of Capacitance, a measure of overall human capacity; and the notion of Creative Symptoms, a way of thinking about protective mechanisms in human systems.

Creative Systems Theory Patterning concepts provide overarching perspective for understanding what makes us who we are and what good choices look like in today's world. They offer a comprehensive set of tools—applicable to both individuals and social systems—for making our way in a culturally mature reality.

The Dilemma of Trajectory and Transitional Absurdity

A couple of further Creative Systems concepts are important to touch on briefly if what we see in our times is to make full sense. The first, what Creative Systems Theory calls the Dilemma of Trajectory, describes how Cultural Maturity's changes involve more than just letting go of one cultural stage and moving to another, how they bring into question the whole developmental orientation that has previously defined growth and truth. The Dilemma of Trajectory makes changes at least similar to those that the concept of Cultural Maturity describes inescapably necessary.

We can describe the Dilemma of Trajectory in multiple ways. Most simply, we can frame it using the language of polarity. Creative Systems Theory delineates how each stage in culture to this point has been defined by greater distinction between polar opposites and a greater general emphasis on difference. (In tribal times, connectedness to nature and tribe was primary; today materiality and individuality prevails.) We can also frame the Dilemma of Trajectory in terms of intelligence's multiplicity. We've evolved from times in which the more creatively germinal aspects of intelligence—the body and the imagination—most informed experience (to be part of a tribe is to know the tribal dances and rituals) to times in which the rational—with a limited contribution from the emotional—holds the much larger influence (enter the

Age of Reason). We can also describe this evolution in terms of culture's story—how it has taken us from times in which archetypally feminine influences ruled to times in which the archetypally masculine is the defining presence.

In our time, this organizing trajectory has reached an extreme: Truth has come to be defined almost exclusively by difference (for example, we view objective and subjective as wholly separate worlds); we equate rationality with understanding; and extreme archetypally masculine values prevail (such as those of the marketplace and science). The Dilemma of Trajectory alerts us to the danger of going further in this direction. Indeed, in an important sense, it stops being an option. We would not do well if we lost what remaining connection we have with nature, or bodies, or the more receptive aspects of experience that form the basis of human relationship. Continuing our current trajectory would irretrievably alienate us from aspects of who we are that are essential to being human.

So what are we to do? We could go back—a proposal at least implied in certain kinds of social advocacy. But going back is not any more likely to get us where we need to go. Unless there is a further option, the human experiment could be at an end. By reconciling the Dilemma of Trajectory, Integrative Meta-perspective offers a possible way forward. And it is a way forward that points toward an essential kind of human realization and fulfillment.

The second additional concept relates to an observation that could seem to prove the concept of Cultural Maturity wrong. A lot that we see in today's world appears to be almost the opposite of what the concept predicts—for example, increasing political and social polarization, widespread denial with regard to essential limits-related challenges such as climate change and the extinction of species, and the growing prevalence of authoritarian rule in places where we might have assumed it to be something of the past. Given that we find so much in contemporary human behavior that can seem ludicrous—and often rather scary—it can be hard to believe that getting wiser as a species is a possibility.

It may not be. But it turns out that much of what we see is consistent with the concept of Cultural Maturity. The concept predicts that our times should be characterized not just by new possibility, but also by times of regression and distorted ways of thinking. Creative Systems Theory calls this particular kind of ludicrousness Transitional Absurdity.[7]

New Capacities and Critical Challenges

Creative Systems Theory argues that we will be able to address challenges ahead for the species—and in the process address the Dilemma of Trajectory and confront Transitional Absurdity—only to the degree we can begin to apply the new human capacities that I've described following from Cultural Maturity's cognitive reordering. Noting a few of those challenges and what they will ask of us helps clarify how this is so. With regard to better understanding personality style differences, in each case the more complete kind of self-awareness and the greater capacity for collaboration that comes with such understanding provides support for needed changes.

How can we act morally in a world without obvious moral guideposts? Until very recently, culture in its parental role has provided us with clear moral rules. Our task has been simply to understand and obey those rules. Today, traditional moral guideposts are losing their authority and the moral relativisms that tend to replace them leave us feeling rudderless. We find ourselves in an increasingly complex, change-permeated moral landscape. Cultural Maturity's cognitive changes offer that we might address moral questions with a new

---

[7] I wrote the short book Perspective and Guidance for a Time of Deep Discord: Why We See Such Extreme Social and Political Polarization—and What We Can Do About It (2021, ICD Press) in response to some of today's particularly concerning Transitional Absurdities.

systemic depth and nuance—and, with it, a comfort with uncertainty and complexity, that has not before been an option.

How do we keep from destroying ourselves? I've noted how collective identity through history has depended on dividing our worlds into "chosen people" and "evil others." This way of defining who we are is becoming increasingly problematic, with the nuclear genie now out of the bottle, and terrorism an inescapable threat. Our safety in the long term will depend on bringing greater maturity and sophistication to how we understand our human differences and how we relate to conflict. Integrative Meta-Perspective's systemically encompassing vantage offers the possibility of getting beyond the polarized and polarizing assumptions that have created us-versus-them worlds.

How do we avoid making the planet unlivable? Climate change, global industrialization, and the broader effects of growing human population threaten to make existence on the planet less and less pleasant. It is quite possible that the earth will eventually become unlivable even for us. If we are going to avoid such an outcome, we must step beyond our modern heroic mythology that views limits only as constraints to be overcome. Culturally mature perspective highlights the inherent role of limits in the workings of living systems and helps us engage them in the most creative ways.

In times ahead, how will the requirements of effective leadership change? Today, trust in leadership of all sorts is less than it was at the height of anti-authoritarian rhetoric in the 1960s. We could easily assume—and people have argued—that this modern lack of confidence in leadership reflects something gone terribly wrong—broad failure on the part of leaders, a loss of moral integrity on the part of those being led, or even an impending collapse of society. But if it does, there is little reason to have hope.

The concept of Cultural Maturity offers an explanation that is more optimistic, but also more demanding. It alerts us to the fact that the meaning of leadership is changing—and in all parts of our lives, from the leadership in ourselves needed to make good personal choices, to what is required to effectively lead organizations and nations. Along with altering how we go about making decisions, these changes invite important reflection about possible next chapters in the way we think about governance and how we structure our governmental institutions.

Leadership's new picture is not all positive. Today we reside in an awkward in-between time with these changes. When we do see leadership that begins to reflect culturally mature capacities, people are as likely to attack it as celebrate it. But if the concept of Cultural Maturity is correct, moving forward in how we embody and relate to leadership is both possible and essential.

How will love change in times ahead? Love might seem more a personal concern, less pertinent to big-picture cultural well-being. But certainly the topic is relevant to people's sense of fulfillment. Changes we see today with love are also directly pertinent to what relationships of every kind will require of us in times ahead. Romantic love of the sort symbolized by Romeo and Juliet represented a powerful step forward from what came before it—marriages arranged by one's family or a matchmaker. But it can't be the last chapter in love's story. While we idealize such love as based on individual choice, it was never quite this. Modern romantic love makes the other person our completion—our white knight or fair maiden. Rather than love between whole people, what we have known is "two-halves-make-a-whole" love. Love today challenges us to love as whole beings. Integrative Meta-perspective makes such more Whole-Person love newly possible.[8] A related kind of change is reordering relationships of every sort. In the end, these changes challenge us to rethink not just relationship, but the nature of individual identity—and with this, what it means to choose and to live purposefully.

---

[8] I examine this is a topic in depth in my book On the Evolution of Intimacy: A Brief Exploration Into the Past, Present, and Future of Gender and Love (2019, ICD Press).

What will it mean to use technologies wisely in times ahead? Technological innovations will be key to future advancement. But it is just as important if we are to have a healthy and survivable future that more effectively assess their benefits and identify potential unintended consequences. These might seem like wholly technical tasks. But, in fact, carrying them out with the needed sophistication will require a maturity of perspective that we have not before been capable of. It has been our Modern Age tendency to treat technology as a god. If we continue to do so, our profound capacities as tool makers could eventually be our undoing. Culturally mature perspective helps us get beyond technological gospel thinking and bring the nuance of understanding needed to apply new technologies wisely.

How must we define progress if our actions are to successfully take us forward? In modern times, we have thought of progress as an onward-and-upward trajectory of increasing individuality and material achievement. While this definition has served us well, it cannot continue to do so going forward, for multiple reasons. Beyond the fact that it is not environmentally sustainable, it should prove less and less successful at giving our lives purpose. Compelling pictures of advancement must take into account the full measure of human needs—not just individual accomplishment and material accumulation, but also human relationships, creativity, the health of our bodies, our larger sense of connectedness in life, and much more.

There is a further critical reason why progress's past definition cannot continue to serve us, which I have just touched on. The Dilemma of Trajectory describes how continuing on as we have would sever us from aspects of who we are that are critical to being human. If this conclusion is accurate, it is not just that clinging to progress's familiar definition would be unwise: Doing so has stopped being an option. Our future depends on defining progress in more systemically complete ways.

As these multiple challenges make clear, like it or not we live in times that ask a lot of us. The important recognition is that, whatever the origins of today's increasingly demanding challenges, with sufficient courage and persistence Cultural Maturity works as an antidote.

Looking at the Evidence

Radical notions like Creative Systems Theory's application of a creative frame and the concept of Cultural Maturity require strong evidence. Here we've seen how Creative Systems Theory's developmental framework—whether we approach it through the lens of polarity or through the evolution of intelligence—provides valuable conceptual perspective. We've also looked at how the fact that Cultural Maturity's changes make needed new capacities possible supports the conclusion that something like what the concept describes will at least be necessary. In addition, we've seen how more specific notions like the Dilemma of Trajectory and Transitional Absurdity are consistent with what a creative frame predicts and makes the need for something at least similar to what the concept of Cultural Maturity describes impossible to escape.

There are other kinds of evidence for the power of a creative frame. For example, in my overarching book Creative Systems Theory, I describe how its application lets us answer questions that have always left us baffled, indeed many quandaries of the "eternal" sort. It turns out that we need Integrative Meta-perspective not just to answer such questions, but to ask them in helpful ways. Some examples that I touch on in the book: How do we reconcile the experience of free will with what logically seems a deterministic world? Are the beliefs of science and religion merely different, or do they represent parts of a larger picture? And how do we best understand the human species 'place in the larger scheme of things?

More specifically with regard to the concept of Cultural Maturity, for me the most compelling evidence that its thesis is correct is the simplest. I don't see another way of framing the human task that is consistent with a healthy and vital future. Indeed, I don't see another way of framing the human task that is ultimately survivable. If I have not missed something important, Cultural Maturity becomes the only option going forward, the only game in town.

An observation implied in Creative Systems Theory's developmental picture provides further support for Cultural Maturity's significance, if it is correct. Cultural Maturity's changes may do more than provide an effective response to today's immediate challenges. They may offer a basic blueprint for right thought and action applicable far into humanity's future. We can think of them as ultimate human achievement.

INDEX

A

Albert Einstein, 3, 20
archetypally feminine, 5, 11, 12, 24, 38, 48, 68, 76, 81, 114, 115, 176, 183
archetypally masculine, 5, 11, 12, 44, 48, 68, 77, 81, 114, 176, 183

B

big-picture perspective, 2
Bimodal patterns, 66
blindnesses, ix, 18, 31, 59, 71, 75, 89
Body intelligence, 23. 58, 145

C

Capacitance, 10, 11, 14, 28, 31, 43, 47, 48, 58, 67, 70, 72, 74, 79, 83, 85, 87, 101, 103, 104, 152, 153, 181
Creative Symptoms, 10, 11, 64, 72, 73, 182
Creative Systems Personality Typology, 4, xi, 1, 2, 6, 7, 15, 16, 65, 72, 98, 137, 142, 150, 151, 158, 163, 167, 181
Creative Systems Personality Typology., xi, 2
Creative Systems Theory, 4, 7, vii, viii, xi, xiii, 1, 2, 4, 5, 8, 10, 11, 12, 15, 16, 17, 18, 48, 64, 65, 71, 72, 79, 81, 88, 89, 101, 102, 115, 116, 123, 137, 152, 153, 154, 157, 158, 159, 160, 161, 162, 163, 164, 165, 166, 167, 168, 170, 171, 172, 173, 176, 177, 180, 181, 182, 184, 188, 189
Cultural Maturity, 4, 7, viii, x, xiii, 7, 8, 12, 14, 18, 62, 64, 75, 76, 77, 81, 84, 86, 149, 158, 160, 161, 162, 163, 164, 165, 166, 167, 168, 169, 170, 171, 175, 179, 180, 182, 183, 184, 185, 186, 188, 189
Cultural Maturity's cognitive reordering, 7, 8, 162, 166, 168, 169, 171, 184
Culturally Mature Leadership, 17

D

Diagnostics, 152
Dillman, Lyn, 6, 98, 122, 123, 137

E

Early Axis Children, 130
Early Terms, 112
Early/Lower/Inners, 26
Early/Lower/Outers, 25
Early/Upper/Outer, 10, 25
Early-Axis, 7, xii, 3, 5, 6, 9, 12, 19, 20, 21, 22, 23, 24, 25, 27, 28, 31, 32, 38, 43, 66, 68, 71, 78, 79, 82, 88, 89, 90, 92, 102, 123, 124, 137, 138, 146, 147, 180
Early-Axis temperament, 3
Experiential Approaches, 7, 106

F

formative process, xii, xiii, 3, 4, 5, 6, 8, 19, 50, 69, 137, 141, 155, 156, 168, 172, 176, 178

H

Horizontal and Vertical Polarity, 148
Horizontal Polarity, 147

I

Inner Aspect, 9, 12, 81
intelligence's creative multiplicity, 7, 15, 22, 143

Intelligence's Creative Multiplicity, 4, 6, 143, 144, 171, 172, 173
intelligence's multiple aspects, 5, 174

J

John Kennedy, 4, 66
Julia Roberts, 4, 53, 67

L

Late Axis Children, 134
Late Terms, 113
Late/Lower/Inner, 56, 60
Late/Lower/Outers, 56, 60
Late/Upper/Inners, 55, 56, 115
Late/Upper/Outers, 55, 115
Late-Axis, 7, xiii, 3, 4, 5, 6, 9, 12, 22, 32, 38, 43, 50, 52, 54, 55, 56, 57, 58, 59, 60, 62, 63, 66, 68, 69, 70, 71, 78, 79, 82, 83, 88, 92, 104, 121, 125, 128, 129, 130, 136, 140, 141, 146, 147, 149, 154, 181
Leonard Bernstein, 4, 53, 117
Lower Pole, 9, 12, 37, 45, 56, 81

M

Middle Axis Children, 132
Middle Terms, 112
Middle/Lower/Outers, 41, 42, 44, 115
Middle/Upper/Inner, 32, 40, 43, 44, 83
Middle/Upper/Outers, 40, 115
Middle-Axis, 7, xii, 3, 5, 6, 9, 12, 26, 34, 36, 38, 39, 40, 42, 43, 44, 45, 47, 48, 49, 66, 70, 71, 78, 82, 83, 88, 91, 97, 102, 104, 116, 121, 124, 127, 128, 129, 132, 134, 135, 139, 140, 144, 146, 147, 181
Middle-Axis temperament, 97
Middle-Axis temperaments, 3, 34, 36
Mother Teresa, 4, 34, 37, 50
Muhammad Ali, 4

O

Outer Aspect, 9, 12, 81

P

Patterning in Space, 2, 10, 40, 71, 83, 101, 104, 105, 114, 115, 144, 145, 146, 147, 157, 162, 181
Patterning in Time, 2, 10, 11, 16, 40, 70, 81, 83, 101, 103, 104, 105, 144, 145, 146, 147, 157, 162, 177, 180
personality diversity, viii, xi
personality structure, 10, 66
personality style, vii, viii, ix, x, xi, xiii, 2, 5, 6, 7, 9, 10, 14, 17, 30, 32, 56, 63, 71, 79, 81, 84, 87, 88, 104, 111, 114, 117, 122, 143, 147, 148, 151, 152, 158, 184
Personality style, vii, 1, 14, 15
Personality Style, 2, 79, 107
personality styles, x, xi, xii, 1, 3, 4, 6, 12, 14, 64, 65, 66, 75, 78, 80, 83, 84, 89, 96, 99, 102, 107, 112, 117, 122, 145, 149, 151, 152, 153
Polar Fallacies, 75, 76, 79
polar juxtapositions, 4, 5
Pre-Axis, 3, 5, 147, 180
Procreative Symmetry, 11

R

Rational intelligence, 38

S

Steve Jobs, 3, 19, 21, 25

T

temperament axes, 10
Teresa Piddington, 122, 137
The Creative Systems Theory Personality Typology, **viii**
Typology's Origins, 64

U

understanding temperament differences in children, 122
Upper Pole, 9, 12, 55, 68, 81, 82, 117

Made in United States
Troutdale, OR
12/11/2023

15750860R00117

NATURES OF FIRE
GOD'S MAGNIFICENT ANGELS

PETER DARCY

Strength of Soul BOOKS

Unless otherwise noted, Scripture texts in this work are taken from the *New American Bible*, revised edition © 2010, 1991, 1986, 1970 Confraternity of Christian Doctrine, Washington, D.C. and are used by permission of the copyright owner. All Rights Reserved. No part of the *New American Bible* may be reproduced in any form without permission in writing from the copyright owner.

Natures of Fire: God's Magnificent Angels, Copyright © 2021 by Peter Darcy. All rights reserved. Published in the United States by Strength of Soul Books. No part of this book may be used or reproduced in any manner whatsoever without written permission except in the case of brief quotations embodied in critical articles and review. For information, address Strength of Soul Books, P. O. Box 346, Port Salerno, Florida 34992.

Books and materials published by Strength of Soul Books may be purchased for mentoring, spiritual development, evangelization, and promotional use. Please visit us at www.strengthofsoulbooks.com or contact us at publisher@strengthofsoulbooks.com.

First Edition

Print book ISBN: 978-1-7332654-4-7

eBook ISBN: 978-1-7332654-5-4

Book design by KUHN Design Group

Cover art: Stained glass window angel from St. Ignatius of Antioch Episcopal Church, New York, NY. Courtesy of Robert Fertitta, 2020.